"God created you in His image to live a God kind of life, but sin made that impossible. Then Jesus came on a great rescue mission to provide the great exchange, allowing you to rewrite your story according to God's script. Bruce and Heather Moore show us what such a life looks like. This book has the fragrance of real life. Don't read it if you want to stay the same."

—DANIEL L. AKIN, president, Southeastern Baptist Theological Seminary

"What every leader needs is a way to maximize the potential of others and help people discover the lives God created for them. *Rewritten* shows us how to embrace the story that will change each of our futures. Bruce and Heather have given us a resource to help us take our next steps."

—TONY MORGAN, pastor, author, and consultant (tonymorganlive.com)

"I love this book! *Rewritten* speaks to the heart of every person who questions what to do when experiencing consequences of painful choices. This book has reminded me that God is constantly here, waiting to rewrite my story with grace and healing. Everyone needs to hear this message!"

—ANNE JACKSON, author of *Mad Church Disease*;
blogger, FlowerDust.net

"*Rewritten* is a fresh approach to helping people get back to the stories God intended for their lives. It's also a quick read for any individual and will break people free to serve others in their churches and communities."

—JOHNNY HUNT, pastor, First Baptist Church, Woodstock, Georgia

"Somehow we know: There is something broken, something wrong. Yet there is also something beautiful, something more. Bruce and Heather have captured the concepts of what it means to be created in God's image, what it means to have that image scarred and polluted, and how that image—our story—can be *Rewritten* and rediscovered by God's grace. This book will help you rewrite your story."

—WILLIAM RICE, pastor, Calvary Baptist Church, Clearwater, Florida

ritten

reWritten

Exchanging Your Story for God's Story

BRUCE AND HEATHER MOORE

NAVPRESS

Discipleship Inside Out™

Discipleship Inside Out™

NavPress is the publishing ministry of The Navigators, an international Christian organization and leader in personal spiritual development. NavPress is committed to helping people grow spiritually and enjoy lives of meaning and hope through personal and group resources that are biblically rooted, culturally relevant, and highly practical.

For a free catalog go to www.NavPress.com
or call 1.800.366.7788 in the United States or 1.800.839.4769 in Canada.

ISBN-13: 978-1-61747-192-6

Cover design by Arvid Wallen

Some of the anecdotal illustrations in this book are true to life and are included with the permission of the persons involved. All other illustrations are composites of real situations, and any resemblance to people living or dead is coincidental.

Unless otherwise identified, all Scripture quotations in this publication are taken from the *Holy Bible, New International Version*® (NIV®). Copyright © 1973, 1978, 1984 by Biblica, used by permission of Zondervan. All rights reserved. Other versions used include: the New American Standard Bible® (NASB), Copyright © 1960, 1962, 1963, 1968, 1971, 1972, 1973, 1975, 1977, 1995 by The Lockman Foundation. Used by permission; *THE MESSAGE* (MSG). Copyright © 1993, 1994, 1995, 1996, 2000, 2001, 2002. Used by permission of NavPress Publishing Group; the *Holy Bible*, New Living Translation (NLT), copyright © 1996, 2004. Used by permission of Tyndale House Publishers, Inc., Wheaton, Illinois 60189. All rights reserved; The Holy Bible, English Standard Version (ESV), copyright © 2001 by Crossway Bibles, a division of Good News Publishers. Used by permission. All rights reserved; and the New King James Version (NKJV). Copyright © 1982 by Thomas Nelson, Inc. Used by permission. All rights reserved.

Moore, Bruce.
  Rewritten : exchanging your story for God's story / Bruce and Heather Moore.
    p. cm.
  Includes bibliographical references (p.   ).
  ISBN 978-1-61747-192-6
  1. Christian life. I. Moore, Heather. II. Title.
  BV4501.3.M6544 2012
  248.4—dc23

                        2011051522

Printed in the United States of America

1 2 3 4 5 6 7 8 / 17 16 15 14 13 12

To our redheaded, blue-eyed little girl — this book is for you. May we model *imago dei* so that you see a clear picture of your loving Creator and understand His amazing plans for your life.

CONTENTS

ACKNOWLEDGMENTS

In a world where celebrities sell everything from shaving cream to cars, they also sell books. We are not celebrities, and it is highly unlikely we ever will be. So it is with deep gratitude that we say thank you to NavPress for taking us into the publishing field. We appreciate that NavPress is scouring the evangelical world to find people who have a message but just haven't yet been heard. Thank you a thousand times over to Mike Miller and Rebekah Guzman for allowing our voices to come alive on the written page. Because of you, we are living our dreams!

Liz Heaney, you are a rock star in the publishing world. Thank you for being willing to take on complete novices such as ourselves. You have pushed us to communicate more clearly and taught us how to be better writers. This book would not exist in its current form without you.

Thank you to Martha Moore, who spent countless hours reading the rough draft and gave us encouragement.

Thank you to our family and friends who prayed for us, encouraged us, and lent helping hands in caring for Gwendolyn so we could have time to write. Without your constant prayers and support, we would have surely given up.

Thank you to our church family, Christ Fellowship Tampa. You are a wonderful source of encouragement. We are so blessed to be a part of the movement of God in our church.

Quite possibly, this is the hardest endeavor we have ever undertaken. The writing process has at times been exhilarating and at other times agonizing. During the difficult times, we kept going back to the fact that God Himself gave us the vision for this book years ago. We have diligently tried to take steps of obedience toward writing and publishing. We felt so strongly that God called us to tell our story that we made the decision to write this book whether or not any publisher wanted to print it.

To our Lord and Savior, Jesus Christ, thank You for transforming our hearts and minds as we have sought to understand what it means to be created in Your image. We are eternally grateful to bear Your image. As we mirror and represent You, may a broken world see Your grace and mercy in our lives.

INTRODUCTION

Your life matters. It matters a great deal.

This is a popular sentiment in both the secular and evangelical worlds today. Go to any local bookstore, and you'll see lots of books written about this topic. That being the case, you are probably uncertain about what this book has to offer you. You may be thinking, *Really? Another book on this topic?*

What sets this book apart from the others is that it asks a different set of questions. Many books on this topic ask: What can I do to make my life better? How can I be richer, skinnier, and do better in my career? Right answers to the wrong questions produce only half-baked answers or unsure next steps.

The questions this book encourages you to answer are these:

- Who did God create me to be?
- What is the story God has had for me all along?
- What is keeping me from living out that story?

Truth be told, life will never be satisfying until you know who God created you to be and exchange your story with the story God has for you. You are God's image bearer, which means you

11

have the potential to accomplish something great. So does every person on the face of the earth, because we are all created *imago dei* — in God's image.

Imago dei is a spiritual concept that often gets overlooked. The creation account makes for great children's Sunday school lessons but somehow never makes the leap to adulthood. It's nice to teach a toddler that God created creepy crawly bugs, giant dinosaurs, and tossed a few million stars in the sky. But when that toddler becomes a teen or young adult, what does he or she know about living life in order to reflect God's image? Somehow the concept gets lost in translation, and we live our lives unaware that whatever we are in life — doctor, plumber, stay-at-home mom, code writer, mail carrier — we are first and foremost designed to bear God's image to a world that is broken.

Problem is, most of us are not living the life God created us to live. Most of us have lives that are far from perfect. We are living out stories that are different than what we had dreamed about. We all have areas of our lives that are plagued with internal disappointments, fear, or shame. The great news is that no matter where you are in life, what God desires for you is not just a better version of what you currently have but something altogether new. He designed you for a unique purpose that only you can fulfill. That's why your life matters!

We've attempted to unpack the spiritual truths of *imago dei* and make those truths plain for all to see and understand. We kept in the forefront of our minds individuals who most recently have made commitments to Christ at our church plant, Christ Fellowship Tampa. If we cannot explain what it means to bear God's image and how to live that out in terms young believers can understand, we have not done our job. We don't write for academia but for the men, women, boys, and girls who have yet to learn that they bear the mark of their Creator.

Ultimately, this book is for any person wanting to exchange his or her story for a better one. It is for the twenty-eight-year-old single mom holding down two jobs and wondering when things will get better. It is for the hardworking fifty-five-year-old who lost a job when the company downsized and is wondering when his start-up business will turn a profit. It is for the young professional secretly wondering why success is not more fulfilling.

The first four chapters of *Rewritten* explore what it means to be created in God's image. The remaining chapters discuss how to rewrite a story that's had a rough start. The stories throughout the book are of real people who have experienced life change; in some cases, names have been changed to protect privacy.

In many books, all the discussion questions appear at the end of each chapter. This separates the aha moment from the actual thought or point the author is trying to make. For that reason, the discussion questions in this book, called "Story Builders," appear throughout the chapters. This allows you to read the material and immediately process the application questions.

We hope that whether you read and process this book on your own or with others in a small-group study you live to your full potential by becoming the person God designed you to be. You will want to check out www.RewriteMyStory.com because there you will find additional information, discussion questions, and leadership tips that are not in the book. Think of it as a free bonus or an upgrade to the purchase of the book. Most important, it's a space where you can share your own story!

Our prayer is for this book to motivate you to action. No more sitting on the sofa, wondering why life isn't going the way you'd hoped. No more pity parties. We want *Rewritten* to connect you with your Creator and inspire you to live out the story He has for you.

PART ONE

YOUR STORY

WHAT A LIFE!

With six toddlers all under the age of four running around the house, our daughter just blended in with the herd. After several minutes, I (Bruce) could no longer hear her squeal or laugh. I asked a simple but critically important question: "Where is Gwendolyn?"

On my way to the living room, I passed the front door. It was open.

As soon as I stepped out the door, the winter air hit my lungs. Earlier in the day, ten inches of snow had blanketed the ground, and I knew that Gwendolyn was not properly dressed for the bitterly cold temperature. The darkness of night consumed everything. With all my strength, I yelled for my little girl. No answer.

My heart stopped. I yelled again and again. Off in the distance, I heard a faint voice say, "Daddy."

It was so dark that I could not see her. I yelled to Heather, "I can't see her. Where is she?" Again the faint voice cried, "Daddy."

"Go to the right, go to the right!" Heather screamed.

I ran as fast as I could. All I could hear was the crunch of snow as I ran hard in the dark. At that moment, time was as frozen as the ice surrounding me. I couldn't see my daughter; I yelled her name over and over again. I felt so powerless as a host of questions flashed through my mind: *Why had I not checked to see if the door was locked? Why had I not checked on her more often? What if my carelessness resulted in harm to my daughter?*

My mind raced, wondering how long she could last outside, and in between the thoughts came my silent gasps of *God, help her!* I screamed her name again as the thought of a funeral service passed through my mind. I wondered if she had fallen into the water or was walking down the middle of the road.

Off in the distance, I saw the small figure of my little girl stuck in the snow. With all my might, I ran to scoop her up, rescuing her from the darkness and harsh elements that enveloped her. Overwhelmed with the thought that my choices could have negatively impacted our family, I collapsed in the snow with my little girl.

As I tucked her into a warm bed that night, I couldn't shake the thought of how quickly things can turn a story upside down. My carelessness could have altered my daughter's story, my story, and our entire family's story. I started thinking about what happens when choices take our stories in directions that are different than what we had planned. Can a life story be *Rewritten* once it's gotten off course?

I looked through the window and saw cars moving up and down the street filled with warm passengers unaware that things outside the car just hours earlier could have gone horribly wrong. This must be how most people stuck in a bad story feel. It feels somewhat like a dream but with huge, painful doses of reality. Others are smoothly passing by, completely unaware that your life is going nowhere. How can they be so at ease while the direction of your life has been derailed? Your story was not supposed to go this way. Somebody switched the roles and you ended up becoming the joke, the homeless, the unemployed, the divorced, the overweight, the disillusioned, the underappreciated. Your ideas have become somebody else's early retirement plan. Your friendships have become someone else's connections. Your loyalty was only a one-way street. You're stuck in a job, in a habit, in fear, in the past, and the funeral has started in your mind. What a life! But it is your life.

CREATED FOR MORE

Life can be confusing, especially when we end up becoming the main character in a story we thought only others would live. The truth is, every person's story in some way has been hijacked. Our expectations and dreams have been seized from us, and in at least some area, we want our lives to start over.

Maybe, like Isabella, you are reeling from the choices of someone else wrecking your life. She sat at her kitchen table, gripped by trepidation as she held the envelope in her hands. She knew its contents, and opening the envelope would be like opening Pandora's box. Once those papers saw the light of day, she would forever be labeled with the "D" word. *Divorced*.

How had her life gotten so far off track? After all, she was the good girl—the morally pure girl who waited for, hoped for, and dreamed of the perfect husband. When she met a handsome young man at church with a good career and supportive family, the dream seemed to be coming together. It all went as planned. The courtship turned into an engagement, which turned into a beautiful wedding.

Isabella was still in newly wed bliss, writing thank-you notes for gifts and settling into her new home, when reality hit. The first time her husband did not return her phone call, it didn't faze her. Maybe he was busy at work. But when there were long periods of time when his whereabouts could not be accounted for, the dream began to unravel and the lies were exposed. Her husband of four months had mistresses. Pornography and prescription drugs were their names.

Isabella's life was shrouded in a cloud of confusion that seemed so thick she'd never find her way out. The most minimal task, such as paying the electricity bill or keeping appointments, slipped her mind. No matter how many times she asked, "How did my life get so off track?" nothing seemed to make sense.

Isabella never dreamed in a million years that her life would end up like this, but it did. We live in a world where we bear the scars of others' wrong choices and hurtful words toward us. When we are the victims of someone else's choice, there is a tendency to even think that they have a greater power over our story than our Creator does.

Most of us want a new life story but just don't know how to create one. How do you do it? Make it up as you go? Borrow someone else's idea that may or may not have worked for them?

We have good news for you. You don't have to come up with all the answers yourself. Because your life was created for more, God wants to exchange your story for His story. He is waiting to give you a life do-over. What may seem to be a random list of meaningless tasks, daily routines, and setbacks is actually a carefully crafted plan that is designed to produce an extraordinary outcome.

Imagine how your life would change if you were living to your full capacity, unencumbered by the weight of the past. God's plan for your life would unfold each new day to reveal hope, meaning, purpose, and fulfillment. The direction of your life would be radically altered. And think about all the people you are connected to: family, friends, neighbors, and coworkers. Because you are connected to countless others, imagine how things would change for them as well simply because you are living the story God has for you! The impact of your life could be staggering. Your story can help transform the world. Why settle for a lesser story?

You might think that this sounds impossible to achieve, but God has already placed a story of hope and potential within you. Each of us is a reflection of our Creator's work, and His work is never random. It always has purpose and greatness within it, so each of us has purpose and greatness simply because we were created by God. When God created you, He made you *imago dei*—in the image of God—which means that you are made like Him.

Even more amazing is that His image looks different in each of us. God's image is reflected through our unique personalities and abilities and the assignments He wants to accomplish through us. This makes each of us—including you!—one of a kind. There's not a person on the planet exactly like you. No one has been created with your unique blend of personality traits, gifts, assignments, and sphere of influence. There's a world that needs you to make the contribution only you can make. The difference you make has the opportunity to change things forever.

You may have been told there is nothing special about you. If so, the problem is not you. The world's view of human life is screwed up. What you do with your life matters. It matters a great deal.

THE KEY TO LIVING GOD'S STORY

In life, there are two stories: the one God designed for us, and the one we create for ourselves. Most everyone chooses to live the story he or she creates and then wrestles with the realization that it's not really working. The problem for many of us is that we mistakenly believe we can find meaning apart from God. But when we create our own life stories, it results in dissatisfaction because we are disconnected from the story God has for us. Life will never be satisfying until we know who God created us to be and the story He created for us. Tim can tell you.

He lost control of his car as it sped down a long stretch of a Texas highway. Truth be known, he had lost control of his life long before this. Money was no object and his alcohol, fast cars, and impulsive decisions resulted in a life spiraling out of control. Never satisfied with his current car, he blew through money purchasing faster and better cars. His vehicles weren't merely a means of transportation; they were thrill rides that fed an insatiable appetite to fill the emptiness in his life. Tim was no different when it came to friends; he collected a set of fair-weather friends who stuck around to be the recipients of free meals and adventure. He couldn't accumulate enough to fill the void in his life.

His body recovered from the car crash, but the last-minute exit of his fiancée at their wedding brought a level of pain that Tim had never experienced. He'd never known rejection, as his life was a constant parade of people wanting to be around him. With a broken heart, Tim decided to move to the big city in search of something his money, fast cars, and relationships had not been able to fill. The move was an attempt to erase the pain, and a new city would give him something else to conquer. But the move did not accomplish what he had hoped for. While he moved furniture and unpacked boxes, his thoughts raced to his ex-fiancée, who was on a honeymoon cruise with one of Tim's "friends." Behind his smile, Wayfarer sunglasses, and shiny Audi sports car, Tim was dying on the inside. This was not the story he had signed up for. Life had gone sideways, and he was running out of new ways of reinventing happiness.

What Tim was searching for is in many ways what we all crave. We all desire something we can't put our finger on that will create for us a better story than the one we are currently living, yet most of us are good at masking the painful reality of our own emptiness. We are hollow, so we pack our days full of hobbies, relationships, business deals, and food in a quest to satisfy our appetite for something bigger. In the quiet spaces of life, we hope for a more fulfilling life than the one we are experiencing. We are frustrated because the stories we create for our lives are defective. They don't work.

Tim felt this dissatisfaction, and it eventually drove him to take steps to allow God to rewrite his story. Today he mentors young professionals, helping them reorder priorities in order to develop healthy relationships and successful careers. On a regular basis, we run into people throughout the country who have seen their story *Rewritten* because of Tim's influence in their lives.

As Tim discovered, God loves us too much to leave us with a flawed story. After all, He created us to bear His image and impact a broken world around us. He wants to restore what is missing and exchange your story for His story. There are people, places, events, and choices you have not yet encountered that can change everything. The new story He has planned for you is not a better version of what you have; it is actually the story He has wanted for you all along.

The key to rewriting your story is becoming who you were designed to be and accomplishing the unique assignments God has for you (we'll talk more about these assignments in chapter 6). All of us are most fulfilled when we bear the image of God through the work of Jesus Christ. This keeps us from missing out on the story we are created for. It also enhances the lives of those around us, bringing hope to a broken world.

Within these pages is a message of hope from your Creator that can radically alter how you view your life. The space between emptiness and living to your full potential is the very space God works in. The moment you have exhausted all your plans is the moment God is waiting for. In fact, He waits until we no longer cling to the things we thought could bring our stories to life. That's when God rescues us.

THE RESCUE

A man gasps for air as he wakes up from a nightmare. He is sweaty and dirty, and the stench is like nothing he has ever smelled before. The four walls of a pigpen are his cage. Rich Jewish boys don't hire themselves out as servants, and most certainly not on pig farms. How has he sunk so low?

Alone and far away from family, he longs to return home. The life he once led is so different from the life he has now. A battle rages within him: Has he gone too far to return to the loving home he so hastily left?

Shame floods him as he remembers how he had gotten into his father's face and demanded his share of the inheritance. He'll never forget the shock he felt when his father liquidated the family wealth to meet his demand. He was brazen, yet his father remained so kind. How foolish he had been, wasting his money on partying with fair-weather friends and flattering women who cared nothing for him. When the economic downturn hit, he had blown through most of his money. He'd started selling his possessions and clothes until he was left with only the clothes on his back.

The pains in his stomach overwhelmed him; he never knew it was possible to be that hungry. Starvation put things into perspective. His father offered him partnership into a lucrative family business it took years to build. He wore fine clothes and ate gourmet foods because of his father's love for him. The father gave him everything he needed. Why had he rejected his father's story and thrust his life into a really bad story? He had no ability to sustain the life he created for himself as he squandered the money and was left to be a slave on a pig farm.

So he devised a plan to return home. He would beg his father for forgiveness and ask to work — but not as a rightful son, just as a servant. Maybe, just maybe, his father would have pity on him. He began rehearsing his speech on the way home.

Meanwhile, his father began the day much like he had begun every day since his son left. Before he surveyed the land, gave instructions to his employees, and checked his accounts, he looked out at the dusty road, hoping against hope to see his lost son returning home. Months had turned into years, and the employees didn't know why he wasted his time with such nonsense. No one understood the depth of love he had for his son. His love trumped harsh words and foolish behavior.

The ever-hopeful father looked down the road once again, following it all the way to the edge of a distant hill. Far off he saw someone approaching, by the looks of it a beggar hoping to find a meal. He looked down at the mountain of paperwork to be done, and then something familiar about the man's gait made the father look up again. He did a double take and then a hard squint. For a moment he thought that his eyes must be deceiving him. Was that his child?

Even though the figure was still distant, the father knew in his heart it was his son. He started to run hard and fast toward his boy. The house staff watched as he bolted from his terrace. The field workers looked up as he passed by them in a full sprint.

The desire for speed overcame the desire for dignity as the father flung his coat aside. The closer he got, the bigger his smile.

He finally reached his son and, full of compassion, embraced him. The father hugged his boy, clenching a shirt soaked full of sweat. The embrace lasted for minutes as the tears streamed down both of their faces. The son's last set of designer clothes had been worn every day for months, and all that had been caked on them rubbed off on the father's new attire. The son held on tight; the smell of his father brought back memories of more innocent days as a boy.

The son began the speech. The father interrupted him; after all, the father had not waited all these many years to withhold kindness. He ordered the servants to bring out the best robe to replace the torn rags. He placed a ring on his son's finger and sandals on his feet, bruised from the long journey. He ordered the best calf to be slaughtered for the benefit of the son's empty stomach. Everything that had been stolen, spent, and misused, the father restored. That is what loving fathers do.

The story of the prodigal son is a well-known parable that Jesus told to describe how God treats us when we come to Him broken and in need of forgiveness. When the misery of the story we create for ourselves drives us back to God, He comes running toward us. His forgiveness outruns even our worst wrongdoings. Our sin is no match for His eternal grace and mercy. His grace outruns even our worst choices.

Whether you have outwardly left God or departed in secret, He longs to shower you with forgiveness. However you think He would respond to your current situation, you have to realize that it is with grace and then even with more grace. This may not be the reaction you imagine, but it is the response you will get. This may not be the God you expected, but it is the God you have. You have a loving God who is always focusing not so much on what you are at this moment but on what you can become, not so much on where you've been but on where you can go.

Why would any of us turn from a God like this? Like the prodigal son, we strike out to get what we want in life. We assume we can create a better life for ourselves than the one God has for us. We may know that God is loving, but we distrust that His plan for our lives is actually better. God doesn't give us what we want at the moment we want it because He knows it can destroy us. When we push to get what God is graciously withholding from us, it opens the door to sin.

Story Builders

- Read the story of the prodigal son in Luke 15:11-32. What about this story resonates with you? How has creating your own story caused your life to go sideways?
- The good news is that God is waiting to rescue you from all of your sins. Look up Psalm 65:3 and 103:10 and commit them to memory. The next time you are in need of a rescue, recite them to God and ask for His help.

The world is messed up. Everywhere we look, there are things that have no business being there. But it was not always this way, which begs the question:

HOW DID WE GET HERE, ANYWAY?

When God made everything, it was in order, correct, and good. The world was at peace. There was no stealing, murder, poverty, hunger, self-abuse, or betrayal. Neither was there adultery, insanity, pride, selfishness, or unreasonableness. Things have changed. Perfection has become polluted.

We all have observed these toxins in others, and we've seen some of them in ourselves as well. Many of these have impacted us in a personal way. We have been hurt from a father's abandonment, a mother's fear, or the treacherousness of someone's choice. We have cried and asked, "Don't they care?" We dislike the impact of a messed-up world on us or on anyone else.

When we think that God is not giving us everything we deserve, it opens the door to sin because we'll do anything to get back what we think is ours. For instance, a father believes a lie that he can find a better lover, leaving a mom and a child to fend for themselves. A businessman believes that he deserves more money, so he deceives investors and creates heartache for thousands of families. We have seen sin in others, and we have lived it out firsthand.

Humankind has been sinning since the beginning, since the dreadful day when Adam and Eve were deceived into thinking that God had deprived them of something special. Adam and Eve took what was not theirs because they believed that God was withholding something good from them. He had told them that they could eat of all the trees in the garden but one. *When the woman saw that the fruit of the tree was good for food and pleasing to the eye, and also desirable for gaining wisdom, she took some and ate it. She also gave some to her husband, who was with her, and he ate it.*[1]

THE DEVASTATION

Adam and Eve's disobedience is known as the Fall, the moment in time when humanity became separated from a holy God. Through their disobedience, sin entered into the world. Thus, from the moment we are born, we are sinful. *Just as sin entered the world through one man, and death through sin, and in this way death came to all men, because all sinned.*[2]

The same thing that tripped up Adam and Eve trips us up. We strike out to get what we want, and our lives start to go off the rails because our plans are rarely God's plans for our lives. Given a few weeks, months, or years, even our best strategies somehow come back to bite us. They are coated on the outside with all that seems nice and noble, and they are embedded on the inside with something corrupt. This is always the ending to stories we create ourselves.

Even as the two of us are writing this book, we are reaping the consequences of this in our own lives. Our rented thousand-square-foot townhome grows smaller and smaller each day. We have prayed for the opportunity to purchase a home, and the search has been a frustrating and disappointing experience. In the last twelve months, we have looked at countless homes and placed contracts on six houses. Each contract has either been rejected or fallen through. On one contract, we were the highest bidder by $12,000. However, another couple got the house because they were an all-cash buyer. Another time, we had an accepted contract, only to be notified that the owner decided to declare personal bankruptcy and the courts seized the house. After a string of broken contracts, we made the decision to put the house hunt on hold for a while.

While we sat in a Whole Foods café, I (Heather) got an e-mail from our real estate agent about a hot deal on a home that had just come on the market. The location and price were great. My heart leaped. I shut my laptop and said, "Bruce, I want this house. Let's go look at it right now!" Within twenty-four hours, we placed a contract on the home with a large escrow check to ensure that no one else outbid us. I was tired of the house search and even wearier of not getting what I wanted. I was determined to make something happen, and that is where our story went sideways.

What was supposed to be a simple contract has turned into four different home inspections and countless meetings with contractors to bid out the renovations. During the title work, it was discovered that the bank illegally foreclosed on the previous owner! The bank has taken the home off the market and, to top it all off, does not want to refund us the cost of inspections. This tangled legal mess and the weeks of multiple phone calls, e-mails, and text messages between our realtor, the bank, and us has drained us. It has hijacked our emotions and energy. We are reaping the consequences of being unwilling to accept God's plan for our family and striking out on our own to get what we want. We are feeling the weight of what happens when you write your own story.

How quickly sin can overtake us. *Sin is crouching at your door; it desires to have you.*[3] Sin damages and seeks to destroy everything in its path, including you. The horrific effects of sin are threefold:

1. Sin tarnishes the image of God in us. It damages us to the level that we instinctively make wrong choices. It creates the illusion that the stories we create will actually work out on their own.

2. Sin won't leave us alone. It would be one thing if sin lured us into making a wrong choice and then left us alone. But our sin chases after us. It accuses us. Our sins speak against us. *Our offenses are many in your sight, and our sins testify against us.*[4] Again, Scripture says, *Although our sins testify against us, O LORD, do something for the sake of your name. For our backsliding is great; we have sinned against you.*[5] Sin lures us into making wrong choices and then runs after us with guilt and shame.

3. Sin prevents us from understanding God's design for our lives. Sin keeps us from understanding the next step in our story because it blocks our relationship with God. It blinds us to the opportunities around us and prevents us from living up to our full potential. It dims our spiritual perception, leaving us to stumble through decisions we normally would have seen with clarity. *Your bad behavior blinds you to all this. Your sins keep my blessings at a distance.*[6] Sin keeps us from seeing how God is orchestrating the events of our everyday lives.

Sin traps us. When it does, anxiety, fear, guilt, and shame become themes in our story. Meanwhile, we battle it out with our guilty conscience. We justify our actions, defend our decisions. The dark side of sin is that it not only leaves a sting but also can be addictive, seducing us to try and conceal it. So we lust when no one is looking, or we hate with a smile on our face. We are deceived into thinking we can manage our sin. In reality, we are trapped in a flawed story. But God does not leave us in our misery. He wants to reclaim us from the effects of sin and the grip it has on our lives.

~~Story~~ Builders

- What visible effects of sin do you see in your life (fear, anger, bitterness, gossip, and so on)?

- How have the effects of sin chased after you? How have they held you back?
- Read Psalm 66:18 and Isaiah 59:2 and commit them to memory. How has sin kept you from hearing from God? How has this impacted your ability to make decisions and take the next steps in life?

GOD IS ALL ABOUT THE REWRITE

If you have ever been overwhelmed by your inability to overcome an addiction or habit, hated yourself for something you did, or longed to be something you were not and had no idea how to become what you wanted to be, you need to know that there is hope. God is not an absentee father. He does not leave us to muddle through life, carving out the best story we can for ourselves. As His image bearers, we are too valuable to be left with a flawed story, so God pursues us to restore our relationship with Him and use us to our full potential.

God is always inviting people into a greater story than they are currently living. Jesus met a woman whose story was broken. She had taken the bait from many a man that her life was not worth more than a few temporal thrills. She ended up with a broken heart and a flawed story. This woman had no idea she was created in the image of a holy God. He had great plans for her life, amazing goals to accomplish, and dreams to be dreamed. Because she didn't know who she was created to be, she fell for a perfectly packaged lie. Each lover might have phrased it differently, but each one was convincing enough that she abandoned all hope of living with value and worth in exchange for the immediate fulfillment of the lover's desires. Not a fair trade, and not a wise investment in her own future.

But that changed the moment this woman met the one Person who knew exactly what she was created to be. At a well in the heat of day, she met the only One who could free her. She met the only Man who could exchange her broken life for a fresh story.[7]

Jesus wants to do the same for us. He offers us an opportunity to have a new life and a transformed story. The only way for God to restore our story is for us to have an encounter with Jesus Christ, not just in salvation but also as we choose to live life committed to the things that will change our stories.

God could have abandoned the whole rescue process. He could have thought, *I've been betrayed too many times; they have messed up the planet and each other way too often*. But He didn't. He loves us too much to allow us to remain flawed, so He graciously sent His Son to remove our sin and give us the power to rewrite our stories. *He is so rich in kindness and grace that he purchased our freedom with the blood of his Son and forgave our sins.*[8] Jesus Christ lived a sinless life. He died a cruel death on the cross; dead just three days, He rose from the grave to conquer sin for all humanity. *Jesus Christ rescued us from this evil world we're in by offering himself as a sacrifice for our sins. God's plan is that we all experience that rescue.*[9]

The story of the gospel does not just end with Jesus' victory over sin and death; it also includes His restorative work in our lives. "The purpose of God in saving a man or a woman is to make that person more like the Lord Jesus Christ. The Lord is not interested nearly in saving you, keeping you out of hell and taking you to heaven when you die. His purpose is much wider and deeper than providing salvation nearly as a means of escaping punishment and entering into bliss at the end of life."[10]

How God rewrites our lives and exchanges our stories for His story starts at the moment of salvation, but it continues as God transforms our lives through the work of Jesus Christ. Our former way of life no longer has to rule us. Instead, little by little, God begins the difficult work of refining our character and making us look more and more like Him. God gives us the chance to respond to five life-changing opportunities: forgiveness, fulfilling our assignments, generosity, humility, and suffering. (We'll talk more about this in part 3.) We all deal with each of these issues at some point in life. Each of these life opportunities allows us to reflect our Creator in a greater way and offers us a chance to rewrite our stories. With each life opportunity, God reveals to us more of His story for our lives and the potential for what we can become if we trust Him to author our future.

~~Story~~ Builders

- You might be asking, *How do I know God wants to rescue me?* Psalm 18:19 says that God delights in you. No matter your past, you are never too far gone!
- Read John 4:1-42 to see how the woman at the well was changed through a personal encounter with Jesus. How has your life been changed as a result of your relationship with Him?
- If you want a personal relationship with Jesus Christ, go to www.RewriteMyStory.com for a step-by-step explanation.

ritten: reWritten

PART TWO

GOD'S STORY

REFLECTING THE
IMAGE OF GOD

Several years ago, I received a Facebook message from a college friend I had not talked to in years. What he wrote stunned me:

> May 6 at 6:17 p.m.
> Hey, Bruce,
>
> You may not remember me but I cannot tell you how many times I have told congregations about you over the last twenty years. Your heart for the Lord was always so evident, even while I was going through my own days of rebellion. I saw your life and admired the joy and ease you found with people and with the Lord. You will never know what a positive impact that had on my life! Thanks for living that before me and so many others who really were paying attention.
>
> All the best,
> B. P.

I stared at the message in disbelief. My friend was referring to a period in my life when I was struggling and depressed. How was it possible that I could have had such a positive impact on anyone during such a dark period?

At the time, I was an eighteen-year-old college student, scared about being two thousand miles from home, and unsure of myself. I certainly didn't think I had anything to offer anyone else or that my life would make much of a difference. Fear was my constant friend, and many days I wrestled with God in prayer to remove the level of depression I felt. Hardly an afternoon went by that I didn't go to my dorm room and just sleep, my one legal and moral remedy for dealing with the unsettled pain I felt. Counseling didn't help, and I sank further and further into a pit of despair. Every day I would get up and pray, *God, I can't get through today without You. Show me what to do and help me see people the way You see them.* It was a prayer of desperation.

So you can imagine my shock when my friend shared that there were things I did and said during this time that had been impacting him for the last twenty years—so much so that he had retold my story to thousands. I suddenly realized, *My story is bigger than I had thought. Its impact reaches far beyond what I can imagine!*

My daily prayer of dependence on God had made all the difference. God answered my prayer and showed me what to do as He helped me see others the way He did. What I didn't know then is that people couldn't see all the junk I was going through because they saw God working in me and through me. With each step I took, there was a piece of me that was reconnecting to who God created me to be.

When a coed came to me for relationship advice, I saw her differently than how her arrogant boyfriend saw her. I could see that she had not been created to meet the need of someone else's every whim. I listened to her story and offered her a tissue and some Scripture verses.

When I entered the lunchroom, I often invited students to sit with me who were socially awkward and didn't have many friends. God had opened my eyes to the reality that the lunchroom is a terrible place to sit alone.

When I saw someone struggling with the course work, I invited that person to be in my study group. I made it a point to encourage and help that person do his or her best.

At the time, these acts of compassion seemed insignificant, but when we are mirroring God's image to someone else, that is never the case. Through my actions, I was reflecting God's image. I was living the way I had been created to live. My choices and actions helped others see something of God's character in me.

Do you realize that every encounter with another person is an opportunity for you to give that individual a glimpse of what God thinks about him or her? People desperately need us to be the expression of God's love, compassion, and grace. When people see God's image in us, it gives them an understanding of who He is.

We were meant to live this way, yet many of us live completely unaffected by the fact that we bear God's image. We don't realize that our lives are the conduit of hope to a broken world in need of that same hope. We fail to understand that our lives are intricately connected to our Creator. Imagine how different your life would be if every decision you made, every thought you contemplated, and every word you spoke arose from the conviction that your life matters greatly because you are created *imago dei*: in His image.

In order to better understand what being an image bearer means and how important your life really is, we need to go all the way back to the start of history in Genesis 1:1 — to the beginning.

YOUR STORY AND GOD'S STORY

What is the earliest memory you have? Think really hard. Eagerly waiting at the door for the arrival of Mom or Dad? A faint recollection of a favorite toy? Some memories capture a feeling, such as the time you first experienced fear or heard a roaring thunderstorm.

Our earliest experiences are important to most of us. Where we come from defines who we are: *I am the son of . . . My aunt is named . . . My town makes . . . In my neighborhood, we always . . .* Where we come from brings a sense of security and significance to our lives because it helps us answer the ultimate questions: *Do I belong? Does my life really matter?* To not understand our origin produces questions that leave fear, insecurity, and heartache.

Oftentimes when we meet someone new, we ask, "Where are you from?" It is not merely a superficial question. We ask the question because the answer can give us insight and information about the individual. It is a natural longing in all of us to know where we come from, which is why we often see adults who were adopted as children on a quest to find their birth parents. Understanding our beginning frames the foundation for how we view ourselves and, ultimately, how we live our lives. Where we come from sets in motion where we are going and leads us to who we will become.

Yet none of us can remember our own birth story. Even so, family and friends often describe it to us. Even though they are not our own memories, we accept the recollections as truth. However, all of our stories begin earlier than even others have told us.

Your story was brought into existence by Someone who thought of you from the beginning of time. You are intricately connected to the God of creation. Your story is one of a kind. There is no one like you on this planet, nor will there ever be. You have been created with a purpose that only you can accomplish.

No other person has the same set of talents or abilities. No one else has the same connections and relationships you have. That's why we can say that you have the potential to make a difference that only you can make. That's why your life matters.

What's even more significant is that God created you to resemble Him. This was His plan for you from the beginning of time: *God created man in his own image, in the image of God he created him; male and female he created them.*[1] God formed both man and woman in His image. Every person on the planet resembles God, and that means you. You are made in His likeness; you carry within you many of the same characteristics He possesses.

~~Story~~ Builders

- What are some of your earliest memories? How have they defined your life?
- Have you been the recipient of someone's reflecting God's love, kindness, or grace to you? What were the circumstances, and how did that impact you?

WHAT DOES IT MEAN?

So what exactly does it mean that we mirror God's image and have some of His characteristics? After all, only God can bring forth a sky that unfolds into measureless galaxies and fashion brilliant stars infinite in number. He alone can orchestrate the rising and falling of vast oceans filled with brightly colored fish and sea creatures. God commanded the sky, sea, land, animals, and plants into being. He spoke the words "Let there be," and each of these things appeared.[2]

After making the elements and the sky and various creatures, God was not finished. He made a man and a woman. Above all the natural wonders of the world stands the creation of humans in His likeness. When God created man and woman, He marked them with His image. To bear His image is like having your very own internal tattoo. Nothing else in creation possesses God's character. Animals are made *by* God, but only humans are made *like* God. We are not God, but we along with every single person on the face of the earth mirror God in some way. We mirror or reflect Him in ways beyond physical characteristics.

For example, God has placed within you the capacity to love Him and others, express thoughts, and make choices. You resemble Him in that you have the ability to reason. You can create things of worth. You have the power to feel emotion. You express yourself through language and can communicate with Him and others. These are gifts from a gracious God. No matter your ethnicity, age, or gender, to be human means to be marked by God.

When you mirror God, people see His character in your life, relationships, and choices. When this happens, they are touched in a way that changes them and alters their lives and future. They may be seeing God like they have never seen nor experienced Him before. This may sound far-reaching, but it's true. As you become who God intends you to be, God is more visible to others, and people get a clearer picture of God through you.

The way we often resemble our parents gives us a small picture of how we can take after God. Like my father, I'm skilled in everything that does not require a screwdriver. When Heather and I first got married, I attempted to put together a bookcase. I glued all the wood pegs in the wrong places, and all of my attempts at getting the bookcase to stand failed. I eventually gave up and placed the leaning bookcase up against the trash bin at our apartment with a sign that read, "FREE." A couple of weeks later, my neighbor thanked me for the new bookcase. Heather's dad, on the other hand, can make and engineer almost anything, just like his father had. When our daughter was born, my father-in-law picked up a fallen tree, planed his own lumber, and built a solid-wood chest and changing table for her. It is a work of art.

Both of us, my father-in-law and I, resemble our fathers.

Just as we resemble in mannerisms, expressions, and inherited abilities those we are physically related to, we are all more like our heavenly Father than we realize. We possess many of His same characteristics. We have all been tattooed, yet most of us don't even know it.

~~Story~~ Builders

- Read the Creation story in Genesis 1.
- What did you learn about God? About yourself?
- What unique tattoos (gifts, natural talents, experiences) has God given you?
- In what ways does your character need to be more like God's character? How would developing those character traits in your life impact your story?

GOD VALUES YOU

Because we are created in God's image, it also means every person who has ever lived and every person yet to be born possesses value simply because he or she lives and draws breath.

His focus is on helping you become who you are designed to be. He graciously wants to complete what He started in you. *He who has begun a good work in you will complete it until the day of Jesus Christ.*[3]

You might not think God really loves you. You might even think there are reasons why He shouldn't.

However, your story is actually about a God who wants His best for you. He is interested in all the things that comprise your life because you are valuable to Him. Even though there are around seven billion people on Earth,[4] God's thoughts are of you. Astonishing.

> *O LORD, You have searched me and known me.*
> *You know my sitting down and my rising up;*
> *You understand my thought afar off.*
> *You comprehend my path and my lying down,*
> *And are acquainted with all my ways.*
> *For there is not a word on my tongue,*
> *But behold, O LORD, You know it altogether.*[5]

God knows your daily activity and is aware of your thoughts. God knows the words you speak before you speak them. He is keenly aware of you. Actually, He knows your story better than you know it yourself.

He is not satisfied to leave you where you are because you are too precious to Him. In fact, He thinks so much of you that He uses you to reflect that value to others.

We see this truth reflected in the way Jesus treated the adulterous woman.[6] Jesus was in the temple teaching a great crowd of people when the religious leaders, known as the Scribes and Pharisees, threw her at His feet as He was teaching. They were very specific with their words. They wanted Jesus to know that the woman was caught in the "very act" of adultery. Of course, this theatrical performance was meant to embarrass and humiliate the woman. Imagine if your greatest sin was announced publicly before a large crowd of people.

Everyone in the temple knew that for the offense of adultery the law dictated a penalty: death. The religious leaders wanted to trick Jesus. They had no concern for the woman; she was simply a means to an end. They said, *Teacher, this woman was caught in adultery, in the very act. Now Moses, in the law, commanded us that such should be stoned. But what do You say?*[7]

Silence. He never answered their question. Instead, He told them, *If any one of you is without sin, let him be the first to throw a stone at her.*[8] Her accusers left one by one, and Jesus was left alone with the woman. Look at what Jesus said next:

> *"Woman, where are they? Has no one condemned you?"*
>
> *"No one, sir," she said.*
>
> *"Then neither do I condemn you," Jesus declared.*[9] *"Go and sin no more."*[10]

Jesus did not condemn the woman. He knew her past — where she had been and what she had done. But His thoughts were of her future. His thoughts were of what she could become.

The Scribes and the Pharisees had thrown the woman at the feet of Jesus, but their act of prideful contempt resulted in her being in the best place she could ever hope to be: at the feet of the very One who created her. No doubt Jesus had treated her like no other man had treated her before: valued. Jesus' act of mercy and grace was a reflection of God's love and grace toward her, and it imparted her with value in a society that said that her life was of no value whatsoever. God is all about mercy and grace, and when we treat others in a similar manner, we are reflecting His image and letting them know that their lives have value.

We recently met another woman who desperately needed to hear that her life has value. Mary makes a living stripping. She was raised by a single mom in a home with a constant flow of men in and out the front door. "It was like our home had a revolving door," she told us. Left alone a lot, Mary was not encouraged to do homework or dream about achieving much in life. The large hand-me-down Sony TV acted as her only companion while her mom worked long days. After too many school days missed and one too many fights, Mary decided school wasn't for her.

Never receiving affirmation or value, Mary did what many young girls do in similar situations: sought to manufacture the feelings of belonging, value, and worth she so desperately longed for. With no education in a bad economy, Mary found the job search discouraging. "A friend of a friend told me I could make good money dancing. Finally, someone noticed me. Someone thought I'd be good at something," Mary said as tears filled her eyes. "The problem is, I bring in so much money that I can't quit, and my boss is threatening me if I do." Mary was trapped in a world where the only value she had was to make her boss money and please men who treated her as if she were disposable. She did not know worth or value as a child, and now in young adulthood those qualities were just as elusive. She told us, "Pray I can get out of dancing and back to school."

As Mary told us her story, we cringed inside, thinking, *Mary, you have been created for so much more. How is it you have gone your whole life and no one told you this?* Each week after church, we looked for her in order to speak to her and pray with her. It was our way of showing value to someone who desperately needed to see herself as her Creator sees her.

Over time, simply because we reflected in a small way the love He has for her, Mary began to understand the value God placed on her. She started coming to church regularly and looking for us. She began inviting friends to attend with her, always making sure to introduce them to us. Mary had begun to realize how valuable she is to God, and this led her to inviting others who needed to hear the same message. She wanted to give others the opportunity to get a glimpse of what God thinks of them. It's staggering to think that when we realize how valuable we are to God, we can, in turn, help others understand how valuable they are to Him. So don't give up on anyone; most important, don't give up on yourself! Even though you might be stuck in bad circumstances or have a past that haunts you, you need to know that God has created you to bear value. Every person has value and worth by virtue of being God's image bearer. That's why every person on the face of the planet has the potential to live better and positively impact other people's stories for good.

Do you realize that God is rooting for you? *If God is for us, who can be against us?*[11] He has desires and hopes for your life. *I know the thoughts that I think toward you, says the LORD, thoughts of peace and not of evil, to give you a future and a hope.*[12]

~~Story~~ Builders

- Read John 8:1-11. What strikes you the most about this story? What stands out about how Jesus responded to the woman?

- How does the fact that God is thinking about your future impact your understanding of who He has created you to be?
- How can you reflect God's character and show value to those around you? Think of someone who needs to know he or she is valued. Pray for that person now. Do something this week to show him or her value.

WORTHY OF BLESSINGS

There is one characteristic of God's that is easy to overlook: the desire to bless those He values. When God created humankind, He made a lush garden for them to call home. Adam and Eve were in perfect harmony with nature. The ecosystem was functioning as designed. No animal species were in danger of extinction. The inhabitants of the garden had never experienced the fury of a natural disaster or the sorrow of death. They lived in a perfect world.

The next thing God did was extraordinary, and it gives us great insight to His character. As if He hadn't given Adam and Eve enough, *God blessed them.*[13] Think about it: The perfect God created a perfect world. Why did He bless them? What more could they need? The blessing is less about them and more about God. He blessed them simply because that is who God is.

God does something similar with you. You are His creation, and He wants to bless you because He thinks you are worth it! Blessings follow worth.

We see this reflection of God's character in everyday life often. We give our time, attention, and resources toward the things we deem to have worth. For example, one day while I (Bruce) was driving home after a long, hard day, the thought crossed my mind that our daughter would love a balloon. I stopped at a store to buy a balloon—not because Gwendolyn earned it but because I love my daughter and naturally want to bless her.

In turn, when we bless others, we are showing off God to a world broken by sin. We are reflecting His image to others. Those around us are blessed by seeing His character through our lives. We are blessed to be a blessing.

Case in point: We live in a quiet neighborhood, and I (Heather) was not expecting any visitors to drop by, so I was surprised by the midday knock on the front door. A young man and his mom (who was mentally impaired and wheelchair-bound) were at my front door. Bruce and I had met them briefly not long after they had moved in. The young man was a full-time caretaker to his mom, and they had no car or family in the area.

The man stood in my doorway fighting back tears. They were in a difficult situation. He recounted a long story of a dispute with the landlord that resulted in the electrical power in their apartment getting turned off. Consequently, they couldn't operate his mom's medical machinery or motorized wheelchair. From the look of fear etched on his face and panic in his voice, I knew this was not a con. So desperate was he that he was willing to stand before a virtual stranger and ask for help. He had scraped together enough money to get the electricity turned back on, but he needed a ride to the electric company to straighten out the mess. To make matters worse, he had to get there within the next hour in order for the power to be turned back on before the long holiday week-end hit. He had already spent a large portion of the day going from house to house, recounting the story and looking for a ride. I was his last resort.

As I stood in the doorway listening, God whispered to me, "I created him. He's mine and he needs help." My mind raced.

My baby was upstairs sleeping, I had no wheelchair lift, and there was no way I could lift the weight of her body into my car. In addition, I had an appointment scheduled across town as soon as Gwendolyn woke up from her nap. The situation seemed somewhat out of my control. I expressed concern over his plight and told him I was unable to help.

As soon as I shut the door, I could not shake the sinking feeling. You know that feeling you get in the pit of your stomach when you know you messed up or missed the opportunity? There in my doorway stood a young man bearing the image of God, asking a fellow image bearer for help. And what was my response? No.

At that moment, I wanted to crawl under a rock, kick myself, or both!

Fighting back the tears, I prayed, *God, what is it that I can do to help?* The words *change bowl* came into my mind. I ran to the buffet and pulled out a bowl that Bruce throws his loose change into each day. When the bowl is full, we count out the change and take it to the bank to exchange for bills. It's our rainy-day fund.

I turned the bowl upside down. Coins rolled out on the floor. I could tell by the amount of clanging of the metal coins falling against each other that it was a large amount of money. I started counting the quarters first. *Lord, please let there be enough for a taxi ride*, I pleaded while counting. Just the quarters alone came to $50. It was more than enough for the man to take a taxi ride to the electric company.

I ran to the door and flung it open, holding up the baggie bulging with coins. There he was walking home, head hung low as if defeated by life. I yelled, "Taxi, taxi!" God had given me the ability to step into his need with a blessing. I was overwhelmed with the opportunity to show worth and value to this young man and his mother.

God's ultimate purpose is to glorify Himself through the work of Jesus Christ in our lives. When we are given opportunities to reflect the character of Christ to others, it brings hope to those in need. When we bless others, we mirror God to a broken and hurting world. God created us to be a blessing to others; that's just part of what it means to be His image bearers. God gives each of us hundreds, if not thousands, of opportunities to represent Him. These encounters matter because God designed for them to matter. You were made to bless others; it is how you are designed.

Story Builders

- In a notebook, keep a written record of all of God's blessings in your life for seven full days. What are some of your unexpected blessings?
- Share your blessings by logging on to www.RewriteMyStory.com.
- Every person's story has something within it that can offer hope and encouragement to others. What do you have to offer that will bless others? (For example, you could write a note of encouragement to someone going through a difficult season of life, text a Scripture verse to a friend, or take a friend to coffee and share about a time in your life when God answered a prayer or met a deep personal need. When others see and hear how God has worked in your life, they are encouraged that God can do the same in their lives.)
- How does knowing that you are uniquely created with value and worth impact how you view God and yourself?
- God's blessings are abundant. Here are just a few examples: Psalm 3:8; 5:12; 34:8; Matthew 5:3-10. Choose one verse

to commit to memory and use as a reminder for the next time you think God's blessings are distant from your life.

WHAT'S NEXT FOR YOUR STORY?

As we've said, being created in God's image means that you both mirror His image and represent His image in specific ways. In this chapter, we've explored how we mirror God's image and how our lives have value because we are *imago dei*. In the next chapter, we'll look at what it means that we represent God's image and why what we do with our lives matters.

REPRESENTING THE IMAGE OF GOD

Because you are created in the image of God, your life has been designed to represent His interests. When you feel the urge to give to a stranger in need, to go out of your way to serve someone, to help others succeed in their jobs, or to bring helpful change to an organization, this is not by accident. You have that thought or desire because God put it in you. He has chosen you to represent Him, and through you He is setting the stage to make this world a better place. Each time you accept His invitation, He is also rewriting your story. With every step you take, God is exchanging the direction of your time, focus, and energy for something better.

Nothing you do is insignificant. You are God's representative, and through you God works out His purposes on earth. Consequently, one choice, one spoken word, can create a ripple effect that will change people you know, everyone they know, and everyone those people know. In you, others have the potential to see God, and what they experience in the process is what they have always hoped for: a Creator who loves them enough to get involved in their stories. When you take on the assignments God gives you, people encounter a loving God who thinks much of them but is unwilling to leave them in their own mess. The world is longing for you to take on the specific assignments God has selected for you.

Hannah Mae, a college grad, got selected one day. She felt the urge to make the world a better place by challenging people to live differently. This passion led her, along with several college friends, to raise awareness about poverty through The October Dress Project. The idea is to wear one outfit for an entire month in order to de-emphasize personal materialism and emphasize that most people in the rest of the world have only a few clothing items because they live in extreme poverty. When people spend less time, energy, and money on their clothing, they are free to be more generous with their resources in order to care for the needs of others.

Hannah Mae and her friends posted about their experience on Facebook and on blog sites, inspiring others to do the same and to live with less so those with less can live with more. Hannah Mae is creating a ripple effect. What started out as four college friends caring about global issues and doing something about it has turned into an inspiring campaign that now thousands of women participate in each year. Hannah Mae knows that she alone can't cure the global issues of poverty, but she can live differently and inspire others to live simply and give generously. Born out of her project experience, Hannah Mae has adopted the motto "Live simply so others can simply live." Today she teaches English to Burmese refugees and serves in an inner-city ministry providing food and clothes to needy families. Hannah Mae is doing exactly what she is designed to do: By being creative and by caring for the needs of others, she is exhibiting God's image to a messed-up world.

YOU ARE AN ARTIST

Being creative is one of the primary ways we represent God. While most of us aren't a Van Gogh or Ansel Adams, as image bearers, we inherited God's ability to create. We have an adventurousness that causes us to want to do things—to accomplish something significant. God has created us in His image so that we may complete tasks and assignments and be a part of things much bigger than ourselves.[1]

This has been true from the beginning. The very first man, Adam, was given a task that enabled his creativity to be used to its fullest: naming creatures he had never before seen. *[God] brought [the creatures] to the man to see what he would name them; and whatever the man called each living creature, that was its name.*[2] So when Adam saw a large creature wallowing in the mud, perhaps the first word that came to his mind was *hippopotamus*. When he saw off in the distance a creature with a strangely long neck eating from the treetops, maybe he said to himself, *Oh, that's a giraffe!*

Because God is a Creator and people represent His image, it follows that every person has some creativity. Every one of us in some way is an artist, from Carole Beal of Five Acre Field pottery studios, who uses her bare hands and lumps of clay to create functional art, to the stories told in the pictures of self-taught photographers Carrie Wildes and Darin Crofton, to the guys at Cappy's Pizzeria in Seminole Heights, who have combined the perfect crust recipe and mastered the topping-to-crust ratio to create the best pizza on the planet. Each of these people is an artist, capable of creating things of value. We all have a Creator God who made us in His likeness to do the same: create. No wonder the Scriptures say, *Whatever you do or say, do it as a representative of the Lord Jesus.*[3]

We all, whether we acknowledge it or not, by the very excellence of our craft, reflect the glory and character of God.[4]

Every time you dream of making something better, of bringing a solution to a problem, of creating a new way of doing something, you are representing God's image. Your dreams of making life better have been birthed in the heart of God. Your dreams are only the start of what He wants to do in you; He has so much more in mind than you can imagine. *God can do anything, you know—far more than you could ever imagine or guess or request in your wildest dreams!*[5]

When you see someone else's potential, forgive people who have hurt you, help someone who has fallen on hard times, or come up with new ideas on how to solve someone's financial or relationship challenges, you are creatively representing God's image to the world, which sets in motion something amazing. When you do these things, God funnels His limitless power through you on those people and it overturns the past, heals the present, and transforms the future. His transforming power penetrates the circumstance and puts into motion what has been immovable.

Here's the great thing about creativity: it does not require a lot of money or an Ivy League education for God to care for others through you. All it requires is creatively using what God has already placed within you and has already made available to you.

We love the story of how Jesus healed a man blind from birth, because it illustrates this truth. Here's what happened. Jesus was walking down the road and saw the blind man. The man had never known the brilliance of a bright blue sky on a cloudless day, nor was he able to look deep into the eyes of those who loved him.

It is not surprising that Jesus, full of compassion, moved toward the blind man. We expect Jesus to be full of grace and mercy. We expect Him to heal the sick, make the lame walk, and help the blind to see. But what we don't expect is how He healed the man. *He spat on the ground and made clay with the saliva; and He anointed the eyes of the blind man with the clay. And He said to him, "Go, wash in the pool of Siloam." . . . So he went and washed, and came back seeing.*[6]

Dirt and spit. Really? Jesus could have laid hands on the man. He could have healed the man from afar. He could have prayed over him. He could have called down a legion of angels to announce the healing. He could have done any of a hundred different things, but He didn't. The plan: Grab some dirt, add some spit, and a blind man can see.

Not to trivialize the man's healing — it is nothing short of a miracle — but notice what Jesus used for the healing: the resources at His fingertips. The dirt didn't have the healing power; that came from God alone. But Jesus used dirt. We too can use what is around us to bring hope to a broken world.

So look around you. What is at your fingertips? What is at your disposal, even if it seems trivial? How can it be used to bring hope to others?

Maybe you are a stay-at-home mom with a college degree in math or science. You could use your degree to tutor a child struggling in math. Even one hour a week could impact that child's outlook on learning and bolster his or her confidence.

Maybe you think you have no abilities or gifts, but because you are holding this book in your hands, we know you can read. You could offer to host a children's story time at your local library. By choosing inspiring stories to read, you could singlehandedly introduce kids to positive role models.

Maybe you are good at baking or encouraging or fixing things or planning parties or rallying people to a cause or pulling the neighborhood kids into a flag-football game. Such abilities are more important than you may think they are. They are at your fingertips because they are being handed off to you by God to share with others.

Before launching Christ Fellowship in 2011, we decided to be more than a church in the city; we desired to be a church *for* the city. And our city had lots of needs. Every day it seemed that more and more people were standing on street corners asking for food, money, or a job. Standing on the street corner was not just for the homeless anymore. Unemployment was high. The housing market stunk. People were hurting. The problem of hunger and poverty was huge and our church did not have the resources to eliminate these issues. However, we were not going to ignore the problem simply because we could not cure it.

We looked around. We asked ourselves, *What do we have at our fingertips to help this problem? How can we creatively use what we have to serve our city?* We have a large kitchen on our church property, and we have people who are caring and loving, so we combined the two, and a ministry called Feed the City was born. We cook and prepackage meals in the church kitchen and then hand-deliver them to people on street corners, at open-air laundromats, and in parks and housing communities. In the first year of Christ Fellowship's existence, we served thousands of meals, filling empty stomachs and touching hurting souls. Each person who receives a meal sees a glimpse of God's love. Does Feed the City cure the issue of hunger for the entire city? No. But it does provide an unexpected source of hope and love, one meal at a time, to those in need.

God wants you to fulfill an assignment that will enable you to represent Him to the world. Instead of living for only yourself and then dying, you have been called to work on God's behalf. Through you, He can create an answer for some task, problem, or opportunity. You are not just taking up space on earth; you are "actually in the process right now of creating a new world in which future generations will live for better or for worse."[7] So look at the people around you. What needs do they have that you could help meet?

~~Story~~ Builders

- Read Genesis 2. It continues our in-depth look into the Creation account and offers us insight into God's character. What do you learn about God? What specific assignments did He give Adam and Eve?
- What specific assignments has He given you? How can you infuse creativity into those assignments? (For example, maybe you created an organizational system that changed how your coworkers access information. Maybe you developed a chart to track your child's progress in household chores and homework.)
- John 9 gives the entire account of Jesus' healing the blind man. Take the time to read this passage. Then reflect on what things, even if ordinary or trivial, are at your fingertips. How might you use them to represent God to others?
- Has something in your life prevented you from creating? From dreaming about your future? What can you do today to begin living with creativity?

- Memorize 1 Corinthians 2:9. Whatever your biggest dreams are in life, God has something even bigger for you.

YOU ARE CREATED TO CARE

The other primary way we represent God in the world is by caring for others. People in every culture and nation have this desire to care for those around them. You can find wonderful parents around the globe. There are individuals in Third World countries living on pennies who make it their business to care for family members and friends. People who have no affiliation to a church or religion run organizations that help the less fortunate.

From the beginning of time, God designed us to care for those around us. He blessed the first man and woman and said to them, *Be fruitful and increase in number; fill the earth and subdue it. Rule over the fish of the sea and the birds of the air and over every living creature that moves on the ground. . . . The Lord God took the man and put him in the Garden of Eden to work it and take care of it.*[8] To care is to represent God's interests here on earth.

Compassion for others begins in the heart of God and is woven into the fabric of who we are as His image bearers. Being a part of something bigger than ourselves captivates our emotions and motivates us because it is how we were designed to live. How is it that Oprah's Angel Network and Bono's ONE campaign have crossed cultural barriers and mobilized hundreds of thousands of people into action? Sure, Oprah and Bono are both celebrities and have huge fan bases, but their ability to mobilize armies of do-gooders goes way beyond fame. When they ask people to help, love, and care for others, people respond because the call to do good and make something happen resonates within each of us.

When we care for others, things happen.

Things happened for our friend Valerie when we cared. Her life was hanging by a fragile thread the day our church reached out to her. After years of drug abuse and prostitution, Valerie experienced for the first time what she had never known: someone who loved her without wanting anything in return. Through a ministry that helps people work through life issues, she found love and acceptance from those who looked past who she had been and instead cared about who she could become. Valerie also discovered that she was designed to be in a relationship with God. Each week she sits in church as a new creation, receiving love and acceptance. We have prayed with Valerie, offered her rides to church, and helped her with her family.

Because we cared, Valerie is now caring for the needs of others. Recently, she participated in our Feed the City ministry, offering food to the hungry and hurting. Normally, we send teams out to pre-assigned places in the city with the greatest needs. Valerie asked if she could take her team to feed men and women living in a homeless camp where she once lived. Her team members watched as Valerie, a former drug abuser and prostitute, cared for and ministered to people who were just like she used to be. Valerie, a new creation by the work of Jesus Christ, represented God through her actions that day.

Live creatively, friends. . . . Stoop down and reach out to those who are oppressed. Share their burdens, and so complete Christ's law. If you think you are too good for that, you are badly deceived.[9] There is one thing about this verse we can take to the bank: We must help lighten the load of people's messes and mistakes. Simple as that: People are hurting, and we get to love and care for them.

In order to make this happen, we have to set aside our own agendas. We have to give up some luxuries in order to help provide school clothes and backpacks to needy children. We have to reorder our priorities in order to have margin in our schedule to influence people.

When we think about people who give to others with no thought of themselves, we think of our friend Don, who traded his position as the president of a $1.6-billion company in order to lead a nonprofit group that helps businesspeople learn how to experience success. We think of Paul, a talented attorney who spends hours each month helping a mentally handicapped man. And then there are Bruce's parents, who for years lived well below their means so they could support organizations helping people in Third World countries. Our friend Greg has taught us how to give more than anyone we know; he has given to the needy and invested in people who will never know his name.

So where do you start? The Scriptures teach us *we are God's workmanship, created in Christ Jesus to do good works, which God prepared in advance for us to do.*[10] God is already in the process of preparing ways for you to represent the gospel by caring for and loving others. Here are five different types of assignments that will allow you to care for others.

1. Giving to the needy

Be careful not to do your "acts of righteousness" before men, to be seen by them. If you do, you will have no reward from your Father in heaven. So when you give to the needy, do not announce it with trumpets, as the hypocrites do in the synagogues and on the streets, to be honored by men. I tell you the truth, they have received their reward in full. But when you give to the needy, do not let your left hand know what your right hand is doing, so that your giving may be in secret. Then your Father, who sees what is done in secret, will reward you.[11]

2. Loving your enemies

You have heard that it was said, "Love your neighbor and hate your enemy." But I tell you: Love your enemies and pray for those who persecute you, that you may be sons of your Father in heaven. He causes his sun to rise on the evil and the good, and sends rain on the righteous and the unrighteous. If you love those who love you, what reward will you get? Are not even the tax collectors doing that? And if you greet only your brothers, what are you doing more than others? Do not even pagans do that? Be perfect, therefore, as your heavenly Father is perfect.[12]

"If your enemy is hungry, feed him; if he is thirsty, give him something to drink. In doing this, you will heap burning coals on his head." Do not be overcome by evil, but overcome evil with good.[13]

3. Giving spontaneously

What good is it, dear brothers and sisters, if you say you have faith but don't show it by your actions? Can that kind of faith save anyone? Suppose you see a brother or sister who has no food or clothing, and you say, "Good-bye and have a good day; stay warm and eat well"—but then you don't give that person any food or clothing. What good does that do?[14]

4. Sharing your talents and gifts

Each one should use whatever gift he has received to serve others, faithfully administering God's grace in its various forms.[15]

All this is from God, who reconciled us to himself through Christ and gave us the ministry of reconciliation.[16]

Whatever other commandment there may be [is] summed up in this one rule: "Love your neighbor as yourself." Love does no harm to its neighbor. Therefore love is the fulfillment of the law.[17]

5. Serving God

Serve wholeheartedly, as if you were serving the Lord, not men, because you know that the Lord will reward everyone for whatever good he does.[18]

The King will say to those on his right, "Come, you who are blessed by my Father; take your inheritance, the kingdom prepared for you since the creation of the world. For I was hungry and you gave me something to eat, I was thirsty and you gave me something to drink, I was a stranger and you invited me in, I needed clothes and you clothed me, I was sick and you looked after me, I was in prison and you came to visit me." Then the righteous will answer him, "Lord, when did we see you hungry and feed you, or thirsty and give you something to drink? When did we see you a stranger and invite you in, or needing clothes and clothe you? When did we see you sick or in prison and go to visit you?" The King will reply, "I tell you the truth, whatever you did for one of the least of these brothers of mine, you did for me."[19]

Sign up to work with the two-year-olds at your church. Send a gift to the person you dislike the most. Double tip, just because. Teach a single parent a new skill to help him or her get out of poverty. Or leverage the thing you're really good at doing in order to help change someone's future career.

When you complete an assignment, it will leave you with the desire to do more, and it will likely inspire someone else to care for others as well.

~~Story~~ Builders

- Have you been the recipient of a kind and loving act? How was God's character revealed to you through that act of love?
- Are there ways of caring in which you can involve your family or neighbors?
- Which one of these five areas are you going to choose this week? Why? What is a practical way to represent God's character in this area?
- Psalm 8:4 is a great reminder that God cares for you. Commit it to memory for the next time you question God's care and love for you.
- Share your experiences of caring for others at www .RewriteMyStory.com. It will encourage others to start their own adventures as well.

There is a world of people waiting for you to embrace their lives, problems, and potential. What a waste it would be for an image bearer not to care for others. God has embedded His image in you, so don't miss the opportunities to represent Him: a wave at the neighbor, a quick smile at the kids at the park as you pass by, changing someone's flat tire in the rain. Each of these ordinary tasks is an opportunity to represent God's image and infuse someone's life with a ray of hope. Ask God to show you how He wants you to represent Him in the world.

When you don't live out of your design, even your best moments cannot fill the hole in your life. However, God wants to rewrite your life story, not merely so that you can live the life you were created to live but so that a broken world can see something of God in you. What you have discarded and written off in the past is actually part of God's plan for rewriting your story and exchanging your story for His.

In the next section of the book, we'll examine five life opportunities God can use to exchange your story for His. These are opportunities to respond to life experiences such as forgiveness, fulfilling your assignments, generosity, humility, and suffering. Your response gives you the chance to more fully mirror and represent God's image and, in the process, live the story God has for you.

PART THREE

THE EXCHANGE

REWRITING YOUR STORY THROUGH FORGIVENESS

If you have been mistreated, hurt, or betrayed, at some point you will have the chance to rewrite your story through forgiveness. Whatever you do, don't pass up this opportunity. Most people do, and they never feel released from the hurt; they stay anchored to the past. Every time you choose to not forgive someone, you attach that person and the event to your life and slow down God's process of transformation in you. Forgiveness frees you up and moves your life forward. It gives you the opportunity to exchange your story for God's story. Just ask Christopher.

The business Christopher had started was born out of sheer determination and hard work. It started out small but grew quickly. He was making a mark in the business world and in the community, but what really brought deep satisfaction to his life was the charity arm of the business. As the company grew, Christopher gave back to the community by investing in a needy area of town. He gave at-risk schoolchildren backpacks filled with school supplies, supported an after-school tutoring program, and invested in community festivals that offered free medical screenings and haircuts.

Another local businessman saw the growth and excitement Christopher's business was generating in the community. He approached Christopher with a proposition that was hard to pass up. Partnering together, they could grow a better business, and Christopher could oversee and expand the charity arm of the company. Agreements were drawn up and signed by both parties.

For a while, things were good. The company's growth sky-rocketed. New customers were coming in hand over fist. With all the growth came money—and lots of it. Christopher didn't notice it at first, but the money began to influence his partner's business philosophy. Then overnight, things changed. His partner began having meetings without him, and he also took an exorbitant salary. Employees were redeployed out of Christopher's area. Under the partner's direction, the company board outvoted and outmaneuvered Christopher on everything. The situation hit a new low when the board voted to shut down the charity arm of the company, crushing all of Christopher's dreams and hopes of making his community a better place. Then the inevitable happened: He was given his pink slip and told to clean out his office.

Though the blow was emotional, it had a physical impact on his body. Even while he was just sitting and watching TV, deep furrows etched his brow. During mealtime conversations, Christopher was slow to join in. It was as though he were living in slow motion. "Everything I worked for has been taken from me. I have been hoodwinked and didn't even realize it," Christopher lamented.

These thoughts played over and over in his mind. The hurt and betrayal put Christopher in bondage; he could not escape the pain. While everything in his mind screamed, "Get a lawyer and fight this thing!" everything in his heart was telling him to get out from underneath the bondage. Christopher didn't want or need the settlement money; what he wanted was healing from the past and hope for the future, so he did the unthinkable.

He began to return good for evil. He gave his former business partner a gift card to his favorite restaurant for his birthday. When others spoke ill of the business after Christopher's departure, he always spoke words of kindness. When thoughts of anger and hurt flooded his mind, he asked God to bless the business. As Christopher began to do these things, little by little the anger and hurt gave way to forgiveness. Peace filled his life, and he moved forward into his future.

God wants to exchange your hurts for something much better, but, as Christopher's story demonstrates, the exchange requires an unlikely decision: the choice to forgive. If you are stuck in the past, unwilling to forgive those who have hurt you, you will not live out the story God has for you.

Before you put this book down or hurl it across the room because everything within you is screaming, "You have no idea how badly I've been hurt. There is no way I can forgive!" let us reassure you that your story will not be complete without your dealing with the issue of forgiveness. We are not saying it is easy; in fact, we know firsthand the difficulty of forgiveness. But forgiveness is radically freeing and life changing.

God has been forgiving humanity ever since sin entered into the garden. It's a good-versus-evil story. We root for good. It's human nature to pull for the underdog. We are not satisfied if evil wins. That's why we sit spellbound when we hear stories of 9/11 widows and of people who have endured horrible things at the hand of another person yet have chosen to forgive and move on with their lives. Unforgiving people are tethered to the past; forgiving people are the ones in Christ who walk into their future with great hope and peace.

Let's take a closer look at the impact of forgiveness on a story gone bad.

FORGIVENESS GETS GOD'S ATTENTION

When we forgive our offenders, God takes note of us. He likes forgivers because by His very nature, He is the Ultimate Forgiver. So important is the issue of forgiveness that Jesus addressed the subject in His model prayer. This is how God wants us to pray: *Our Father in heaven, hallowed be your name, your kingdom come, your will be done on earth as it is in heaven. Give us today our daily bread. Forgive us our debts, as we also have forgiven our debtors. And lead us not into temptation, but deliver us from the evil one.*[1]

And as if He wants to underscore the point, He follows the prayer with these words: *If you forgive men when they sin against you, your heavenly Father will also forgive you. But if you do not forgive men their sins, your Father will not forgive your sins.*[2]

"When you pray '*Forgive us our debts*' . . . you are asking God to let you off the hook."[3] We don't want to be held accountable for our mess-ups and mistakes. Literally, to forgive means "to send away." God sends away our sins through the work of Jesus Christ on the cross. "Your sins would be cast away from you and you would not be liable for them; instead of your having to pay, God just lets the debt go."[4] *As far as the east is from the west, so far does he remove our transgressions from us.*[5] You are off the hook! When God forgives your sins, they can't be found because God has sent them away.

The challenge for most of us is that this prayer is "forgiveness hardball." We want our own sins erased, but at the same time, we want our offenders to be held accountable for their sins. We like mercy for ourselves and justice for our offenders. "The most natural tendency in the world is to want to get even when someone has offended you. It is as natural as eating or sleeping, and it is instinctual."[6] When we desire forgiveness for ourselves yet demand accountability for those who hurt us, it fosters our own pride and self-righteousness. When we offer forgiveness, it keeps our pride in check.[7] Jesus knew that others would hurt us, so He strongly emphasized the need to forgive. When we do, we mirror God and reflect His mercy and grace to a world that is hopeless without it. Forgiveness is essential if we want to rewrite a bad story; forgiveness gets God's attention.

The model prayer tells us that when we forgive others, God will forgive our own sins. The act of forgiveness invites God to deal with us as we have dealt with others. *God blesses those who are merciful, for they will be shown mercy.*[8] Nothing gets His attention faster than when we show mercy and forgiveness to those who have hurt us. Forgiving those who have harmed us elevates our actions from the natural to the supernatural. To live in the natural realm is an easy thing. It takes nothing more than our own strength and power. To live in the supernatural, however, can be done only through Christ's strength. *I can do all things through Christ who strengthens me.*[9] Forgiveness is not and never will be a natural act, especially when we have been hurt badly. To forgive is a supernatural work. Every time we forgive, we are participating in a miracle.

If you have ever wondered how to forgive, Tom has wondered it a thousand times. Not long after Tom and his wife had their first child, their marriage dissolved. As much as he tried to be fair with his ex-wife, she consistently bullied him. Family money allowed her to keep Tom in the court system for years, fighting for the right to parent his son and spend time with him. Despite numerous court rulings in his favor, Tom barely got to see his son.

Years later, Tom met and married Jill. When we met them, they had just had a new baby. Their lives were happy and fulfilling; however, the constant struggle with Tom's ex-wife was overwhelming. The woman's life goal was to relentlessly inflict pain on Tom.

As we heard the stories and saw the pain on their faces, we knew that Tom and Jill had deep wounds. However, they made a courageous choice to do the unthinkable: They made the choice to forgive Tom's ex-wife. Forgive the woman with the venomous tongue and well-crafted legal schemes? Forgive the woman who tried to steal precious days, weeks, and years from Tom by keeping him from his son? Yes, that is exactly what they did.

Forgiveness is not easy.

For Tom and Jill, it had to be more than a mere mental assent; they needed something tangible that they could do to help them release the pain. They started praying for Tom's ex-wife. Because they were praying, they had the supernatural strength to do some amazing things. They decided to return good for evil by being flexible with the ex-wife when she wanted the son on particular days. She did not return the favor. They were kind with their words; she was harsh and condemning. They spoke no ill of her in front of the son; she was not so careful with her words.

Tom and Jill are reflecting and representing God's image and are teaching their son a powerful lesson about forgiveness. They are a testimony to the fact that when we rely on God, He gives us the strength and power to forgive, even when the person continues to heap hurt upon us.

Tom and Jill's act of forgiveness put them on God's speed dial. He is pouring out blessings on their marriage and other areas of their lives because He took note of their prayers. In a down economy, Tom's career is booming. The situation with the ex-wife could have caused a tension in their marriage, but praying together for her has unified and strengthened their relationship. They have grown in their understanding of God. Forgiveness and God's attention are directly linked!

Had Tom and Jill been unforgiving, their stories would always be wrapped up in something ugly.

Had they been unforgiving, they would have been tethered to the past.

Had they been unforgiving, they would have missed the blessings of God.

Forgiveness unclipped the strings the ex-wife held on them and opened the doors for their future. Forgiveness enabled them to exchange their story for God's story.

Things might be going well in your life right now. There will likely be a time, however, when you need to forgive someone. There will be a situation that brings you to your knees, and it is at that point that you will want God looking out for you. Be forgiving, and you'll be on God's speed dial!

~~Story~~ Builders

- Read Luke 6:36-38. How are mercy and forgiveness linked?
- Have you ever extended forgiveness to others? What blessings did you receive as a result of doing so?
- If your story is stuck or spiraling out of control due to wounds inflicted by another person, your comeback could be around the corner. However, you must be willing to forgive. Before you put this book down to absolve yourself

of having to forgive, let us ask you this: Would you be willing to ask God *if* He wants you to forgive your offenders? Would you at least be willing to read the remainder of the chapter with an open mind?

THE PARTY CRASHER

One reason people have trouble offering forgiveness—and remain stuck in their unfulfilling story—is that they fail to realize their own need for forgiveness. Our ability to forgive others is directly linked to how much we believe that God has forgiven us. If we think God has forgiven us a whole bunch, then we forgive much. If we think our sins are small, then we will have a problem forgiving people who sin greatly against us.

This was a major roadblock in the lives of the religious leaders in Jesus' day. Jesus was invited to eat dinner at Simon the Pharisee's house. As the dinner party was in full swing, an uninvited guest barged into the house. The party crasher was well known around town, but for all the wrong reasons. She was an immoral woman. Because of the services she provided men, she had saved a large sum of money. Perhaps she figured there would be a day when she would no longer be wanted and that a day was coming when men would discard her. So she saved enough money to purchase an alabaster jar of perfume, an extremely prized commodity worth an entire year's wages.

Her job put her in the constant flow of town gossip, and she heard that Jesus was in town. Without hesitation, she grabbed the most valuable thing she owned. She would dare not waste this precious commodity on just any man. After all, what were men to her except a business transaction? No man cared for her mind or heart. She wondered if the things she had heard about Jesus were true. Had she finally found Someone who would care for the deepest needs of her soul?

So she pushed her way past the front door and into the dinner party. You can imagine the double takes as she walked by each guest. Heads turned and people wondered why she was there, when she walked up to the One person she came looking for: Jesus. When she found Him, she fell to her knees and began kissing His feet and washing them with her tears. She pulled out the priceless alabaster jar of perfume and poured out her retirement over His feet.

Simon, the host, was so offended by this act that he questioned Jesus' ability to discern what type of woman was at His feet. Simon said to himself, *If this man were a prophet, he would know who is touching him and what kind of woman she is — that she is a sinner.*[10] Simon's focus was on the woman's sin but not on his own sin. She did not stop kissing Jesus' feet even while Simon insulted her. She didn't even say a word to defend herself.

Jesus found it difficult to stomach Simon's self-righteousness. Because Simon didn't understand, Jesus skillfully told him this parable:

> *"A man loaned money to two people — 500 pieces of silver to one and 50 pieces to the other. But neither of them could repay him, so he kindly forgave them both, canceling their debts. Who do you suppose loved him more after that?"*
>
> *Simon answered, "I suppose the one for whom he canceled the larger debt."*
>
> *"That's right," Jesus said.*[11]

Simon had neglected to grant Jesus the common courtesy of the day by offering to wash off His dusty feet before He entered into the house. The woman, whose tears of gratitude cleaned Jesus' feet, showed up Simon big-time. She knew exactly who and what she was: a sinner. She didn't need any religious leader to point that out. She knew she needed forgiveness for her many sins, and she knew where to find it. She was so consumed with how much she needed forgiveness that she didn't get sidetracked from kissing the feet of Jesus, even as Simon demeaned her in front of the whole crowd. That was why she could ignore the insults of Simon. The insults didn't matter because she was at the feet of Jesus.

Simon, meanwhile, thought he had so few sins that he was not in great need of forgiveness, yet he was quick to criticize others. As Simon's actions show, when someone does not understand the magnitude of his or her own sins, it is impossible for that person to understand forgiveness. We can't extend mercy and understanding to others until we realize our own desperate need of forgiveness.

When we feel we have no need for forgiveness, then we also don't think we need grace. When we think that we have it all together, we will never beg God for help. When we think we have all that we need, we never plead with Him for more. But the truth is this: All of us are in need of God's grace and forgiveness. He extends grace because we are in need of it. He extends forgiveness because we are in need of forgiveness. When we are keenly aware of our own need to be forgiven, we are more open to forgiving others.

~~Story~~ Builders

- Read Luke 7:36-50. Which character in the story are you most like?
- Why is forgiveness so difficult to extend to others?
- Take a moment and ask God to forgive you for any sins in your past or present that haunt you. Get freedom today!

COME BACK TO THE STORY GOD HAS FOR YOU

If your story has gotten stuck or sidetracked due to hurtful words or actions toward you, don't allow the wreckage of unforgiveness to eat up five, ten, or even twenty years of your life. Jesus gives us four steps to move forward in forgiving others: *To you who are willing to listen, I say, love your enemies! Do good to those who hate you. Bless those who curse you. Pray for those who hurt you.*[12] Each of the following steps is essential to seeing the new direction God has created for your life.

Step 1: Love

Step 1 is to love those who hurt us — to show mercy to them the way God has shown mercy to us. When we love our enemies, our perspective begins to change. We see their need for love, and we see how God has placed them in our lives to be the vehicle of His love.

Many times we would rather tag somebody else with this assignment. We might think, *We're not enemies; we just don't get along very well.* We'll create any excuse possible to unhinge ourselves from the obligation of showing love to those who have hurt us. Jesus prefaced His words with the phrase "You who are willing to listen" because not everyone will want to listen. He knows that loving an enemy goes against our human nature. But those who are willing to listen gain the blessing of a comeback story.

Step 2: Do Good to Those Who Hate You

The practical side of forgiveness is to do good toward those who hurt us. Forgiveness can be abstract, but step 2 ensures that we love through action, thus representing God to the world around us through our deeds. This step includes meeting the needs in people's lives, giving a present, or serving those who hurt you in some tangible way. Doing good to our enemies seems foreign because it is the opposite of what we would like to do. In reality, we don't want our enemies to benefit from acts of goodness; we'd rather see them suffer. We don't want to sacrifice for them.

Serving an enemy moves you out of the victim position and catapults you into a position of strength. I (Bruce) learned this years ago when a minister from another church spoke untruths about our church. In the process, some people—most of whom were new to our church—assumed the lies were true and left the church. The lies hurt me. Later, I heard that the minister was having financial problems. I knew I had to do something to help me forgive him, so I prayed about how I could show him love. Instantly, the words "Pay his mortgage" came to mind, so I wrote out a check and sent it to him. I didn't want to do it and it made no sense—and I had to make sacrifices in my budget in order to pay for his mortgage that month—but when that check was written, I was no longer the victim. Instead, I was in the position to receive God's peace and grace. If I had harbored resentment, my story would have been stuck to this man's betrayal and lie.

When we show love in a practical way, our enemy doesn't have the last word. Love moves us to the position of strength.

Step 3: Bless Those Who Curse You

To bless people means using our words to encourage and uplift them, even while they say hurtful things about us. Of course, the last thing we want to do is compliment someone who has hurt us. But it helps to remember that it's likely that your offender is wounded and has never had someone else bless him or her. Hurt people hurt people. People walk through life wounded and, as a result, inflict wounds on others.

Blessing an offender is also "withholding certain facts you know to be true, so as to leave your enemy's reputation unscathed. . . . Total forgiveness sometimes means overlooking what you perceive to be the truth and not letting on about anything that could damage another person."[13] Jesus was constantly looking beyond who people were at that moment and instead focusing on who they were created to be. We bless our offenders by minimizing the details of how they hurt us. We bless those who have hurt us when we reduce the verbiage about their screw-ups and increase our words about their potential.

Step 4: Pray for Those Who Hurt You

When we forgive others, we are classified as a child of God. *Love your enemies and pray for those who persecute you, that you may be sons of your Father in heaven.*[14] Forgiveness takes place as we pray for our offenders. Prayer invites God to work on behalf of people who hurt us. But as we pray, God begins to work in our own lives. Prayer may not change your offender, but it will change you! It has certainly changed me (Bruce).

There was an unexpected knock on my office door. When I opened it, a woman stood before me. As soon as she sat down, she started to weep. She was extremely concerned about the direction of her husband's life. Chad had made some bad investments and was now facing legal action. Serving jail time was a very real possibility for him. She begged for my help.

I won't go into the details about why, but this man had hurt me deeply. Everything within me screamed, *Why should you care about this guy? Don't waste your time on this jerk! Let him get what he deserves.* But before I knew it, I told the woman I would commit to praying and fasting for her husband for an entire week. Even though I had committed to praying and fasting, my heart and attitude were not in the right place because it bothered me that I was giving up something for someone who cared so little for me.

But as I prayed for Chad, God began working in my own heart. I realized I had a greater appetite for the buffet at the local Chinese restaurant than I had for seeing God do a miracle in Chad's life, so I started increasing my prayers for him and the difficult situation he had gotten himself into. I fasted one day, then a second day. By the third day, God had not released me to stop praying, so I continued to fast and pray for ten days. On the tenth day, I felt at peace. I was not surprised when later that day, Chad knocked on my office door. *Here comes the apology*, I thought. When it didn't come, I got frustrated with God. Why had I fasted and prayed for someone who had not changed at all? Then it hit me: I was as stubborn as Chad was in certain areas of my life. No one knew about my sins, but God did, and He was patiently working on me. God had been working on my life for way more than ten days! What right did I have to be so impatient with Chad?

When we first pray for our offenders, our prayers focus on their problems, but over time God deals with our own issues. In this instance, God revealed my own need for His mercy and grace. When I realized my need, I started asking God to show Chad the same grace and mercy He had extended to me. "To truly pray for the one who hurt you means to pray that they will be blessed, that God will show favor to them rather than punish them, that they will prosper in every way. In other words, you pray that they will be dealt with as you want God to deal with you."[15]

It goes against every fiber of our being to pray for those who harm us. It is extremely difficult. Many people are subjected to great tragedies in their childhood. Others experience loss and abandonment that mark their lives forever. Still others have to practice forgiveness on a daily, if not weekly, basis because of their continued connection with an offender. Forgiveness can seem unbearable at times. However, it will set you free from the wounds you bear. If you release your offender from the wounds he or she has inflicted, you'll also be fully released from the power that person has over you.

~~Story~~ Builders

- Forgiveness is not an easy concept to master. It doesn't mean forgetting what has happened to you — that would be abnormal. No one can just erase harmful memories. Forgiveness is something far greater than forgetting. Forgiveness is releasing the offender. When you do, it releases you as well. Consider what these additional verses say about the issue: Romans 12:14; Ephesians 4:32; Colossians 3:13.

GOD REMOVES THE STING

In case you are still unconvinced that forgiveness can exchange your story for God's story, then you need to meet a man named Joseph.

Joseph was born into means as the favorite son of the largest landowner in his area. His father, Jacob, gave him an expensive coat, and that didn't sit well with his older brothers. Their father was always siding with the young Joseph. To top it off, Joseph told his brothers that he'd had dreams in which they were bowing before him, and this made them angry. In a fit of rage, they did something that likely haunted them for years: They sold Joseph to slave traders and concocted a cover-up plan. They soaked his beloved coat in blood to trick their father into believing that his favorite son was dead. Shock, betrayal, and hurt were Joseph's companions as he was hustled into a foreign country and sold to a high-level government official. He worked hard and told himself, *This is the day my dad will come to rescue me*. He knew nothing of the story his brothers had told his dad, and every day he would go to sleep disappointed.

Joseph learned a new language and new customs and was promoted to oversee all of the business and personal investments of his new boss. His industriousness was rewarded with trumped-up charges of rape by his boss's wife. The scorned woman's words betrayed the honest slave, and prison became the repayment for showing loyalty to his master. Betrayal followed Joseph again.

While in prison, he used his discernment from God to interpret dreams. He foretold the future of a political prisoner, and the prisoner agreed to help Joseph upon his release. But the promise was forgotten, and Joseph was once again betrayed.

Yet, despite all the many lies and broken promises, Joseph was able to forgive each of these perpetrators. He waited in prison another two years before seeing God's plan for his life unfold. During this time of waiting, Pharaoh was having one nightmare after another. He asked people what these strange dreams were all about, and no one could figure them out. The reason no one could discern the dreams was because God had selected only one person to interpret the dreams: Joseph. Only Joseph had been given the extra grace to understand what Pharaoh's dreams meant.

After he interpreted Pharaoh's dream, he was released from prison and elevated to the highest post in Egypt. He did not retaliate against any of his betrayers, and when he saw his brothers again, he forgave them for their hateful behavior toward him and offered them grace. Joseph understood forgiveness in such a powerful way that he named his firstborn son Manasseh, which means "God has made me forget all my troubles." The name suggests, "God has removed the sting." Joseph was celebrating the fact that God had removed the sting of all the betrayals he had experienced. Because he was willing to forgive, Joseph made an incredible comeback. His story started with betrayal, and God rewrote it into a grand story of success, power, and significance.[16] (In the next chapter, we'll talk more about how He did this.)

Forgiveness is the first step in rewriting a bad story. When you forgive, a messed-up world sees God's character on display through you and your extension of grace and mercy. Forgiveness releases you from past hurts and launches you into your future. It releases you from spending your time and energy on your offender. It also lays the groundwork for discovering the purpose of your life. No one is more excited about your story than your Creator. He longs for it to unfold and for you to live with complete fulfillment and satisfaction. He has created you for a purpose. Finding your purpose is the next step in rewriting a story that has gone wrong.

~~Story~~ Builders

- Read Joseph's story in Genesis 37, 39, and 40.
- In what ways can you identify with Joseph?
- Has God shown you someone you need to forgive? What is your first step in making the difficult decision to start loving that person, doing good, and blessing and praying for him or her?

REWRITING YOUR STORY THROUGH FULFILLING YOUR ASSIGNMENTS

"Can I speak with you a moment? It's important," Samantha asked between church services. As a pastor, when I hear this phrase I get nervous because it is usually followed by bad news. I braced myself for the worst and listened while Samantha said, "I don't know how to tell you this, and it has never happened to me before, but I believe that God has spoken to me about something."

"Really, what is it?" I replied.

"My husband and I are getting a new car. We have an SUV we were going to use as a trade-in, but God told me we are supposed to give the car to you and Heather." Samantha quickly added, "I shared this with my husband and thought he'd never go for it. When he heard what God was telling me to do, he thought it was a great idea!"

Our car had been in an accident a few weeks before. I told her, "We were praying for a car because ours was totaled." Beaming, Samantha said, "I had no idea you were looking for a car." Over and over, she kept repeating, "I am so excited that God spoke to us!"

No doubt Samantha was happy to help meet a need in our lives, but what she was most excited about was that she had actually heard God's voice and obeyed. The God of the Universe spoke, and He spoke clearly—no puzzles, no riddles, no confusing language that had to be decoded by someone with a religion degree.

What enabled Samantha to hear God's voice so clearly? She had positioned herself to hear from Him. Although she was new to our church, she was serving on a ministry team and active in a small-group Bible study. The combination of serving, worshipping, and studying God's Word prepared her to hear clearly from Him. Samantha was excited because her Creator God had handpicked her to complete an assignment. She found satisfaction in knowing she could hear directly from Him and in doing so become a part of something bigger than herself.

THE ASSIGNMENT

As Samantha discovered, our life stories are most fulfilling when we become who we are designed to be and accomplish the unique assignments God has given us. Our assignments—whether a call to an internal change or an external change—are opportunities to represent God and be obedient to the unique assignments He is giving us. When we fulfill these assignments, it gives our lives purpose and meaning. This is the way God has designed life.

The assignments God gives you are the tasks only you can fulfill. As we pointed out earlier, there is no one on earth like you, nor will there ever be. No one else has your particular personality, unique gifts, or specific set of friends. No one else has been given your individual assignments, and no one but you can fulfill them. You have been created to leave your generation different than you found it. You are not here by accident; therefore, every assignment God has for you to do is important.

After all, why would God create you in His image to represent Him in this world and then hand over to you something unimportant to accomplish? *Eye has not seen, nor ear heard, nor have entered into the heart of man the things which God has prepared for those who love Him.*[1] You cannot imagine the plans that God has for you. His plans for us are always bigger than we understand. We wake up every day in a world where God has preordered the events of the day and allows us to join Him in His work. What an amazing opportunity!

We are God's workmanship, created in Christ Jesus to do good works, which God prepared in advance for us to do.[2] We are God's workmanship, which means we are His creation. Made in the image of God, we are given the ability to do good works through Jesus. These assignments have value because God has been preparing them in advance. He has taken great care in preparing the right circumstances, people, and moment for us to carry out what we are designed to do: bring hope to a broken world. Our assignments have been waiting on us for a while, so they are ours to claim.

When we accept the assignments God gives us, they enable us to fulfill His purpose for us, and they change our stories. The reason they change our stories is because we have a God who wants to bless us for completing His work on earth. God is watching what we do, and He wants to unleash His blessings on us. Like a parent who has been shopping for months to surprise a child for a birthday, God is waiting for the right moment to give to those who carry out His assignments. *How great is the goodness you have stored up for those who fear you. You lavish it on those who*

come to you for protection, blessing them before the watching world.[3]
When we carry out the assignments of God, it not only places us
in the greatest place of blessing but also affirms for us the areas
God likes to bless.

Because fulfilling our assignments has such widespread influence, let's take a look at two ways we find our assignments.

FINDING YOUR ASSIGNMENTS THROUGH GOD'S WORD

When we left Joseph in the previous chapter, he was in the most
difficult place in his story. He'd been sold into slavery, betrayed by
his master's wife, and thrown into prison and forgotten. What
was the purpose in that? With such a bad story, how would he
ever be used by God to make a difference? A look at Joseph's life
gives us hope that God can use even the most desperate story, and
it also gives us insight into ways we can find our assignments.

One thing that strikes us about Joseph is that he took the time
to know God's plans. Three specific instances in Scripture note
that God was *with Joseph,* and we can therefore infer that Joseph
was with God. Once in Potiphar's house and twice in prison, it is
said of Joseph that *the LORD was with him.*[4] The Lord was with
Joseph because he spent time with God.

Think about it: No one else around him was worshipping
God. No one else around him was an Israelite. The only way
Joseph could have known God so intimately was to have spent
time with Him. Joseph took the God of Israel into Potiphar's
house and into the prison. Theirs was a personal relationship.

If you want to know what assignments God has for you, you
too must spend time with God. You are created for a relationship
with God, which means His top priority is to converse with you.

The written Word is the primary way He speaks to us. *All Scripture is God-breathed and is useful for teaching, rebuking, correcting and training in righteousness, so that the man of God may be thoroughly equipped for every good work.*[5]

As we read and interact with the Bible, God prepares us for our assignments. God's Word changes our thoughts, words, and actions. It makes us more aware of where God is working and how He is inviting us to be a part of what He is doing. God's Word is vital to exchanging our own stories for God's story because it shows us what is important for us to accomplish.

It is utterly breathtaking to imagine that the Creator of the Universe speaks directly to us in Scripture. The Bible is not some random collection of God's thoughts as He passes the time up in heaven. Every time you move forward on an assignment God has given to you, it moves you away from your past and rewrites you into your future. Nothing is more exciting in life than to see the trail of fulfilled assignments and know that you are coming back to God's design for you.

There are four questions to help prepare and position you to identify and complete the assignments God has for you. When reading Scripture, consider these questions, as well as the ideas from 2 Timothy 3:16-17.

1. What am I to *know*?

All Scripture is God-breathed and is useful for teaching.

God's Word teaches us what is right and true. It is accurate because it comes straight from the mouth of God. We all get advice from well-meaning people, but only Scripture allows us to know what God says about life issues. Scripture identifies what is important, right, and useful. When we read or listen to Scripture, it keeps us from going down roads that go nowhere and spending time on useless things.

When you read God's Word, ask yourself:

- *What am I to know about this passage?*
- *How should I respond to this life principle?*
- *Is there something in this Scripture that God is asking me to do?*

God is eager for you to know His truth. Expect to hear from Him when you ask these questions. He may reveal to you something that you already know you should be doing. If this happens, realize that obedience is the first step. Before God can give you guidance on anything else, big or small, you must do what He has already revealed to you. Obedience to what you know you should do in one area is the key to understanding your story in another. Why? Because you can't be trusted with the next step if you are unwilling to follow His lead on the first one.

2. What am I to *stop*?

All Scripture is useful for rebuking.

God warns us through His Word about specific actions, attitudes, lifestyles, relationships, and sinful activities. He points out what is unhealthy for our lives. For example:

Stop passing judgment on one another. Instead, make up your mind not to put any stumbling block or obstacle in your brother's way.[6]

Turn from evil and do good.[7]

Turn my eyes away from worthless things; preserve my life according to your word.[8]

Sin puts a barrier between you and God, disrupting your ability to hear clearly from Him about issues that concern your life. Sin prevents you from understanding what assignments God has for you to do. For that reason, God's Word warns us against behaviors that are sinful. The word *rebuke* sounds harsh, but when God's Word encourages you to stop doing something, it is actually a kindness. God is not trying to kill your happiness; He is trying to stop you from wasting your life on things that have no future. When we are willing to stop what is wrong, we are free to experience the good things God intends for us. When we are free of wrong thoughts, words, and actions, God can replace those things with something better.

One of the greatest gifts of God's Word is the understanding of how to avoid pathways that are dead ends: relationship dead ends, business dead ends, and personal dead ends. God's Word shares with us principles for living that keep us from entering into choices that rob us of God's best. We can't see the future, but God knows the future, and He uses His Word to keep us out of danger.

When you read God's Word, ask yourself, *Is there something I need to stop doing?* If He shows you something, ask Him to forgive your wrongdoings.

3. What do I need to *change*?

All Scripture is useful for correcting.

God's Word shows us what we need to change. These are mid-course corrections. These corrections are not as much about stopping a sin as they are about taking corrective steps so we don't miss an opportunity to reflect God's image. Some activities are okay for some people but not for you. For example, you may make a decision to cut back on the number of times you visit a restaurant in order to reduce your debt. Others might forgo buying a new pair of jeans in order to provide backpacks and school supplies for at-risk kids. Some people might even offer their free time to help a coworker excel at work. When you respond to a change that God asks of you, it takes you to another level of understanding in His story for your life. When you read God's Word and feel convicted about altering something in your life, God is actually revising your story. This is part of His revision process.

When you read God's Word, ask yourself:

- *Is there an area of my life that needs change?*
- *What steps can I take to make this change happen?*
- *With this change in my life, am I more able to fulfill my assignments?*

4. What do I need to *start* doing?

All Scripture is useful for training in righteousness so that the man of God may be thoroughly equipped for every good work.

God's Word teaches you to do what is right so that you are prepared for every assignment that comes your way. As you practice what God invites you to do, you become trustworthy for greater opportunities. These opportunities expand your story. When you start doing what is right, God gives you opportunities to influence others and create a better story than you could have written on your own.

The accumulative effect of fulfilling new assignments distances you from your past. Over time it prepares you for the story God has for you. Saying yes to God's Word rewrites the direction of your life.

When you read God's Word, ask yourself:

- *What does this passage tell me are the assignments (good works) God has designed for me?*
- *How can I be prepared and ready to fulfill these assignments?*
- *What open doors do I need to go through in order to fulfill my assignments?*

PUTTING IT ALL TOGETHER

Here's an example of how these questions and ideas work in a person's life.

One Sunday after church, Mary approached me with tears streaming down her face and told me that God had spoken to her. She was new in her faith, but she never missed a worship service. She was also involved in a Bible study for new believers that taught her the basics of reading God's Word, praying, and serving. For the first time in her life, she was *starting* to pray.

After weeks of reading God's Word, she just couldn't shake the discomfort she had about her boyfriend. She *knew* from looking into the Scriptures that living with her boyfriend was not pleasing to God and would eventually hurt their relationship. I encouraged her to ask God what He wanted her to do about the boyfriend and what His plans were for her life. I encouraged her to act on whatever God asked her to do.

Several weeks later, Mary came up to me again, her face beaming with excitement. She said that God asked her to *stop* dating her boyfriend and *change* her lifestyle. She obeyed God's voice by breaking up with the boyfriend and asking him to move out. She said, "I love the Bible! God has something to say to me every time I read it. I am so happy. I feel like God has used this decision to remove some confusion in my life. I have always wanted to help in our church's feeding ministry, but until now I felt there was something blocking me from doing it. I know this is what God wants me to do."

As Mary continued to read God's Word, He continued to speak to her. Months later she approached me again after a worship service. Before she could say anything, I said, "Let me guess: God spoke to you again!" She said, "Yes! I love babies and I heard that the children's director needed more volunteers. I have been serving for weeks. I love how it makes me feel."

And indeed Mary's life did have purpose. God had clearly given her the assignment of working in the nursery, and it was a much bigger task than she imagined it would be. She gave parents the peace of mind that their babies were being cared for, which allowed them to attend worship and, for many, hear a message of hope for the very first time. Mary was using her gifts and passions to represent the interests of God. Because she was fulfilling her assignments, her life had purpose and meaning.

Every opportunity to know, stop, change, or start something in your life is an opportunity to exchange your story for God's story and fulfill the assignments He has for you.

~~Story~~ Builders

- Responding to and putting into practice God's Word brings satisfaction to life. Read Psalm 119:32-35. What assignments have you completed, and how have they impacted others? How did completing an assignment affect your life?
- Is there anything you are involved in on an ongoing basis that would displease God? Ask for God's help in overcoming this issue. Most important, ask for His forgiveness.

- What is an assignment God is training you for? What steps of obedience do you need to take in your life?
- Read Proverbs 21:1 and memorize it this week. God is in control and has no problem directing you in the way you should go.

FINDING YOUR ASSIGNMENTS THROUGH DIFFICULTY

Sometimes God uses the challenges of life to help us understand what He has given us to do. That was certainly true for Joseph. Let's return once again to his story.

One day the Egyptian Pharaoh had a dream that no one could interpret. The political prisoner Joseph had once helped remembered Joseph's discerning abilities and told Pharaoh about him. Suddenly, Joseph was pulled from the dungeon, cleaned up, and taken before Pharaoh. When Pharaoh told him the dream, Joseph interpreted its meaning: Egypt would undergo seven years of great harvest followed by seven years of famine. Joseph told Pharaoh to prepare for the lean years by stockpiling food during the years of plenty. Then, in a complete reversal of fortune, Pharaoh appointed Joseph to oversee this process. He told him, *You shall be over my house, and according to your command all my people shall do homage; only in the throne I will be greater than you.*[9] Amazing. Just minutes prior, Joseph was sitting in prison. Now he was second-in-command over all Egypt and influencing people around that nation.

During the seven years of plenty, Joseph carefully stored up food in great abundance, so much so that it was beyond measure. *When the famine was spread over all the face of the earth, then Joseph opened all the storehouses, and sold [food]. The people of all the earth came to Egypt to buy grain from Joseph, because the famine was severe in all the earth.*[10] No one, rich or poor, had food. Kings of great

nations stood like beggars before Joseph. He was the most powerful man in the world.

The years of hurt and pain had placed Joseph in the position
to fulfill his God-given purpose. Joseph's assignment was to bring
hope to a broken world in the form of food. He did not turn away
the hungry and hurting; he fed the world. It was his destiny. His
gifts and abilities intersected with the purposes of God. Fulfilling
our purposes involves making a difference where it can most be
felt. Our assignment is not as much about ourselves as it is about
being an image bearer who helps repair a world filled with
damaged people and cracked dreams.

Sometimes, like Joseph, we find our assignments as a result of
difficulty. No matter where we turn, doors slam shut. When they
do, many times we're left with one, and only one, option.
Difficulty—although we don't understand it and certainly don't
like it—can lead us to the specific assignment God has for us.
Oftentimes, our assignment is the only thing left that we can do.

That's exactly how it was for Joseph. Sold into slavery, he had
no option but to work for Potiphar. However, God used Joseph's
time as a slave to prepare him for a much larger assignment.
Potiphar put him in charge of the whole house, so much so that
the only decision Potiphar made each day was what to eat. Not
only had Joseph made Potiphar a far wealthier and more respected
man but it was in Potiphar's house that Joseph's character was
tested and his leadership skills developed. Later, when he was
thrown into prison for resisting the unwanted advances of
Potiphar's wife, Joseph had no option but to spend years in jail,
where he was put in charge of the whole prison. The lives of every
prisoner were in his charge. Once again, through this unlikely
assignment, Joseph honed his leadership abilities. But even more
important, the difficulty brought him his next assignment.

That's how life is sometimes. Doors close that we hoped to walk through, and unexpected doors fling wide open. Difficulty ushers us into our next assignment. Had Joseph not encountered so much difficulty in his life, he never would have met the man who recommended him to Pharaoh. On the surface, it seems a terrible tragedy and waste that Joseph was falsely accused and imprisoned, but prison was the preparation for his being able to fulfill the greatest assignment God had for him. The difficulties Joseph faced prepared him for his purpose.

Lest you think this kind of thing doesn't happen in the twenty-first century, we want to tell you another story about how God sometimes uses difficulty so that we might live the story He has planned for us.

Most people would assume that Lydia and Victor have a good life. As young professionals, they both have good jobs and live in a high-end neighborhood. Their impeccably decorated pool home is always open for barbecues and weekend parties. But all the luxuries in the world were not enough to fill the ache in Lydia's heart. She would have traded every beautiful thing in her life for the chance to have a baby.

Unable to get pregnant, she turned to fertility treatments. Her life became a flurry of trips to fertility clinics, self-injected hormones, and medical procedures that left her feeling like nothing more than a pincushion. But as time passed and she did not get pregnant, it was clear that the best doctors and medical treatments could not give her what she so desperately longed for. The door to motherhood seemed closed. Sorrow and heartache were her constant companions.

Hope seemed in sight, however, when a young teenager chose Lydia and Victor over hundreds of other potential parents to adopt her unborn baby. Before they knew it, Lydia and Victor sat on an airplane to meet the birth mom and her family. The face-to-face meeting turned into multiple phone conversations, e-mails, and text messages between Lydia and the teenager throughout the pregnancy. Lydia's excitement grew as she proudly showed off sonogram pictures of her soon-to-be little girl. She meticulously researched and ordered the best baby furniture. The nursery was coming together. Motherhood was in her grasp. Weeks later, life for Lydia and Victor came to a screeching halt when all communication with the birth mom stopped. A phone call from the adoption agency confirmed Lydia's worst nightmare: The birth mom had changed her mind. The bitter taste of their reality loomed over Lydia. Motherhood went unrealized yet again as another door shut before them.

What Lydia did not know was that God was not withholding motherhood from her; He was just aligning all the circumstances for a greater purpose. When doors keep closing, it many times leaves us with one and only one option. All the closed doors in Lydia's life were about to usher her through one big open door.

One day Victor decided to go fishing and went to a local Wal-Mart to pick up some fishing gear, where he met Thomas. The two men struck up a conversation about their love of fishing, and a friendship was born. Weeks later, Thomas was planning a holiday cookout, and he invited both Victor and Lydia. At the cookout, Thomas shared a story about a coworker whose grandchildren lived in another state and were in a hopeless situation. Their father was in prison and their mother had all but abandoned them. The kids had spent their young lives being passed around between family and friends in an effort to find someone to care for and raise them. The story tugged at Lydia's heart, but the conversation got interrupted and never returned to the plight of the two little babies.

Still reeling from the failed adoption, Lydia put on the bravest face she could muster and walked back through the doors of the adoption agency. The director wanted to talk to her about a new opportunity and began to share about two little babies being moved from foster home to foster home because the father was in prison and the mother had abandoned them. She added, "The grandmother is driving to Texas to get the babies." Lydia sat speechless. She thought, *These are the same children Thomas told us about!* And, indeed, they were the very same children.

Two weeks later, Lydia and Victor held their babies for the very first time. The other doors had been closed for the purpose of leaving one door open wide for Lydia to walk through, making her a mom twice over. Difficulty, while we don't understand it and certainly don't like it, is the setup for specific assignments from God.

Story Builders

- Read Joseph's story in Genesis 41. How has difficulty prepared you for open doors?
- It is hard to understand how closed doors are for our benefit. Read Psalm 84:11. God promises to give us everything we need for a wonderful life if we make decisions that please Him. Just because one door closes doesn't mean it won't open at a later time or that other doors won't open.
- Log on to www.RewriteMyStory.com and tell us about how closed doors have led you to some of your best assignments.

God often uses difficulties and His Word to prepare us and change us so that we gain a greater understanding of His purpose for us and identify His assignments. Nothing is more fulfilling than knowing that we are doing exactly what we should be doing and that nothing is out of place in our lives.

REWRITING YOUR STORY THROUGH GENEROSITY

Life had been going along just fine until our Sunday afternoon drives to a Starbucks near downtown Tampa started messing with us. The trip was our way of ending a hectic workday of multiple church services with something fun. Our drives into the city started out as a way to relax, but over time, something significant happened.

As we drove through Tampa, we began to notice that people's needs were quite different from those of folks in the suburbs. We were confronted with homelessness, low-income housing, unemployment, and poorly rated schools. Often we would see groups of young adults sitting in parks or other public places, wasting away their day. We wondered, *Do they have jobs? Has anyone encouraged them to finish school? Do they know they have been created for a purpose—that they have something of value to contribute to the world?* We realized that the people we were seeing were full of untapped potential. These men, women, boys, and girls had not had anyone love them or care about them in a way that reflected the Creator. As we drove home and through the iron gates to our community each week, we couldn't shake the disparity between the two worlds. Ours was so comfortable, and just minutes away from our backyard was a city full of needs. How had we failed to notice? Why had we failed to be generous to fellow image bearers in need?

Over the course of the year, we realized something about ourselves. We were addicted to comfort. Before our Sunday afternoon drives, it was easy to fill our every whim and pass it off as a need. But once confronted with the realities of other people's lives and the difficulties they face, it became harder for us to purchase another Hugo Boss shirt or another designer handbag. We saw that our addiction to comfort impeded our ability to mirror and represent God's image to the world. Meanwhile, accumulating more and more stuff left us so dissatisfied. We were restless for something new and fresh.

The war in our hearts and minds was not to be quieted until the day we got an unexpected phone call. A dying church in the city called Bruce to ask him to become their pastor. The church had one year to live before the lights would be turned off and the doors shut. If this happened, it would communicate to thousands and thousands of people that there is no life or hope to be found in the church. Suddenly, the previous year and our growing unease all made sense. Our story was in need of a rewrite, but not because of a bad story. Quite the opposite. We were in a good story, but God wanted something more for us. He wanted our lives to look more like His. He was calling us to a sacrificial, generous lifestyle. *If you try to hang on to your life, you will lose it. But if you give up your life for my sake, you will save it.*[1]

We said good-bye to a contract on our dream house and traded ministry and friends at a large church for a new church plant. In the worst economy in our lifetimes, we went from a great salary to no salary. We are learning to live with less so that those with less can live with more, and God is exchanging a good story for an even better one. He is enabling us to mirror His image to the hungry and hurting around us. Generosity is the remedy for our addiction.

This new story God allowed us to have let us trust Him at a level we had never experienced before. Our faith in God to provide for our needs gave us great opportunities to rely on Him each month for rent and grocery money. Significantly cutting down shopping trips for new clothes, we funneled money for outreach projects, backpacks, and school supplies for needy kids and started a Feed the City ministry. Generosity removed our focus from ourselves and put it squarely on the needs of others. It rearranged our priorities and gave us God's perspective on the needs of people we were obviously overlooking. Peace and a deep sense of fulfillment have flooded our lives, and we are not the same people we were a year ago. We now know that generosity goes way beyond money into a lifestyle where every part of our lives is available to be used for others.

Just because your story may be going well, it doesn't mean God thinks everything is fine or that you are living the story He has planned for you. God desires to exchange any area of your life that does not properly mirror His image.

~~Story~~ Builders

- Proverbs 11:24-25 tells us how God blesses a generous life. In what ways has God blessed your generosity in the past?
- In what ways is God asking you to be more generous?

MIRRORING OUR GENEROUS GOD

When we are generous with our money, time, and talents, we are mirroring God's image in us, for He is generous and lavish in all He does. He placed each star in the sky and paints each sunset for the enjoyment of eyes that may never fully appreciate them. He gives us life and bestows on us His image. He is liberal and free-handed in all His blessings. It is impossible for any of God's gracious gifts to be scant or given halfheartedly. In fact, His graciousness chases after us:

> My cup runs over. Surely goodness and mercy shall follow me all the days of my life.[2]

> Let all that I am praise the LORD; may I never forget the good things he does for me.[3]

> Blessed be the Lord, who daily loads us with benefits.[4]

Jesus speaks from experience when He says, *It is more blessed to give than to receive.*[5] His assignment was to come into the world not to be served but to serve *and to give his life as a ransom for many.*[6] His acts of generosity always come out of His own sacrifice and are focused on the deepest need of the person. Jesus' greatest act of generosity was to die in our place, and in doing so He bought us back from the devastating effects of sin and restored us to who we are created to be. *[God] saved us, not because of the righteous things we had done, but because of his mercy. . . . He generously poured out the Spirit upon us through Jesus Christ our Savior.*[7] Through Christ's sacrificial generosity, our full potential can be realized.

People are instinctively drawn toward people who display acts of graciousness and kindness. We see this in Jesus' life. People with stories needing a comeback longed for His outpouring of love and compassion. He attracted those who desperately needed to be whole. The woman with a hemorrhage wanted to touch Him, lepers lined the streets to see Him, and tax collectors invited Him to their dinner parties.

Jesus' earthly ministry is one continuous act of generosity. People did not get what they deserved but what He graciously gave them. God urges us to give to others in the same manner: freely, abundantly, and gladly.

> *Remember this: Whoever sows sparingly will also reap sparingly, and whoever sows generously will also reap generously. Each man should give what he has decided in his heart to give, not reluctantly or under compulsion, for God loves a cheerful giver. And God is able to make all grace abound to you, so that in all things at all times, having all that you need, you will abound in every good work.*[8]

Bruce's mom, Clemmie, gave to others in just this way. It was a Sunday night and Clemmie loaded her mentally disabled son, Paul, into the car. Under normal circumstances, they would be heading to church. After all, Clemmie was a pastor's wife and she was expected to attend Sunday evening worship services. However, God had given her an assignment to perform that night, so she and Paul headed to the maternity ward of the hospital.

Sarah, an unmarried teenager who attended Clemmie's church, had just given birth to a beautiful baby girl. No one else was visiting the new mom that night, but Clemmie felt compelled to do so. No matter what anyone said, this teen mom was special and needed someone to believe in her like never before. Clemmie's schedule was packed full raising three children, one of whom required twenty-four-hour attention. Her responsibilities of being a pastor's wife and a pediatrician taking care of patients at the clinic for needy families was a schedule few people could imagine. She felt that her time and life should always be available, though, for the opportunities God placed in front of her. Every time she felt God's nudge, she believed she was representing Him in the lives of others.

When she arrived at the hospital, she prayed with Sarah, gave her a verse of Scripture to encourage her, held the baby, and offered some advice on newborns. Although the two women were years apart, Clemmie committed to keeping the friendship up. She left the hospital thrilled with the possibilities of what God could do through this young mom and her baby.

Clemmie had no idea that her little visit was not so little for Sarah. In fact, it was a huge transfer of love, acceptance, and belief in her future. Clemmie's unexpected act of generosity helped Sarah redefine her life direction. It was the catalyst for this young mom to start thinking about what her life could become and what kind of life her baby could experience. Sarah started dreaming, planning, and working toward her future.

She started her own company designing wedding cakes for the wealthy and baking pastries for high-end clients and eventually creating desserts for one of the top restaurants in the world. Sarah never forgot how Clemmie believed in her when others were filled with doubt. Sarah has become known for her generosity; she looks out for others in need, cares without much caution, and always goes out of her way to give her clients more than they ask for.

When Sarah learned that the two of us were getting married, she begged to design our cake. For our daughter's first birthday, she designed a cake that was so extravagant it could have been featured on the Food Network Channel. Even though Sarah charged us pennies for her elaborate creations, she was overjoyed to be a part of the special events in our lives. Her generosity transported us back to that maternity ward, where Bruce's mom's small act of generosity represented Jesus and impacted an unwed teen mom's life forever. Sarah told us, "The hospital treated me as nothing more than a statistic that was going to go on welfare, but your mom's visit changed everything." Generosity changes people because it is the clearest view of the grace of Jesus and how much He loves us, unrestrained and skimping on nothing.

~~Story~~ Builders

- How has God been generous to you?
- How has His generosity changed your life, circumstances, and outlook on life?
- Read Isaiah 32:8. Think of someone who needs you to extend kindness to them this week. Devise a plan to do it, with no expectation of a returned favor.
- The Bible is full of people who overcame great odds to accomplish something amazing. Read 2 Corinthians 8:1-7 to be inspired. In your estimation, what is keeping you from being more generous? How can you overcome those obstacles?

IT'S ALL ABOUT THE LEFTOVERS

Some people mistakenly think that generosity is for rich people only. Nothing could be further from the truth. Cultivating generosity as a lifestyle has less to do with how much money you have and everything to do with how much you trust God. Generous people trust that God will meet their needs. They don't have to be miserly with what they own because they understand that all they have and all they are belong to God. Givers understand that they are caretakers of what God has entrusted to them and, therefore, are free to graciously dispense to others anything God asks of them.

That was the situation of an impoverished widow Jesus met. Because her husband had died and because women had no way of supporting themselves in those days, this widow dove headlong into poverty. In a world that prized wealth and social status, she was invisible. Her life mattered little. But in her brokenness, she stopped Jesus in His tracks. For a moment in time, she had the undivided attention of the Creator of the Universe, and He made sure all those within an earshot of His voice took notice of her as well. He applauded her actions and in doing so made sure she would be remembered for all eternity.

Jesus was teaching in the synagogue. He was talking to His disciples and something caught His attention. *He looked up and saw the rich putting their gifts into the treasury, and He saw also a certain poor widow putting in two mites.*[9] Because Jesus sat opposite the temple treasury, He saw how much people gave and must have scrutinized the intent of the givers. Jesus notices what people do with their money.

Two mites were nothing, but when Jesus saw the widow toss the coins into the basket, He did a double take. Her sacrificial generosity grabbed His attention because He knew she was hopelessly poor. It moved Him, as her giving looked exactly like the way God gives to us: unrestrained and reckless. No wonder He did a double take.

Her extravagance separated her from all the others who gave that day. *Truly I say to you that this poor widow has put in more than all; for all these out of their abundance have put in offerings for God, but she out of her poverty put in all the livelihood that she had.*[10] The wealthy gave to God out of their surplus; the widow gave all that she had. The rich gave out of their wealth and were merely tipping God. Their offering would not cause them to go without a meal or miss paying a bill. The widow, however, would go to bed hungry and wake up not knowing how her bills would get paid. Hers was a gift of extreme sacrifice. The reason she could give with such generosity was because she knew that God ultimately would take care of her. The same God who invited her to give is the same God who would meet her needs. She knew that God alone was the source of provision for her life.

> *Honor the LORD with your wealth*
> *and with the best part of everything you produce.*
> *Then he will fill your barns with grain,*
> *and your vats will overflow with good wine.*[11]

Jesus was so pleased by the woman's extravagant generosity that He plucked her out of obscurity and lavished praise on her. According to Jesus, her actions redefined generosity. It is not defined by how much people give but by how much they have left over after they give. After the widow gave her two mites, her account was empty. She had given God all she had.

Jesus made a point of what the widow had done because He didn't want us to miss out on seeing what is at the core of God. She was bearing the image of God through generosity, and the scene was all too familiar to Jesus. There is none more generous than His heavenly Father. *God so loved the world, that he gave his only Son.*[12] God loves extravagance in giving because He Himself is a Giver.

As we extend generosity, we are reflecting God's character to those around us, and God blesses our efforts.

~~Story~~ Builders

- Generosity provides an escape from being selfish. What is one thing you can give up, sell, or trade in order to practice being a more generous person? Remember generosity is not about how much you give, but about how much you have left over!

GENEROSITY FUELS GENEROSITY

When we mirror God's generosity, it rewrites both our stories and the story of the person to whom we are giving.

Many people have found that the more they give away their money, time, and talents, the more they crave the new story that is unfolding. Not only that, but the lasting impact of their sacrificial choices inspires others to make similar choices. Generosity ends up rewriting everybody's story because it is an expression of God's generosity to us. When we are generous, we are living the story we were created to live; we are reflecting God to others. We are representing His grace to others, and His grace never leaves anyone unchanged.

This was certainly the case for Edward and the many people his generosity touched. Edward was the heir to one of the largest car dealerships in Texas. His life was privileged. Everything he wanted was at his fingertips: the finest clothes, gourmet imported foods, and the most prestigious schools. His life was planned out, as he was to assume the helm of the business empire. But a trip to Asia to help the less fortunate changed everything—literally.

Returning home, Edward felt empty. What started out as a trip to offer a few American dollars to help the poor with food and medical expenses unlocked something deep within his heart. His first and last thoughts of the day were about the people he met there. Edward was not satisfied with just offering money to help, because he knew that money alone doesn't always solve one's problems. What Edward really wanted was to live in Asia and do something far-reaching by giving his time, energy, thoughts, and emotions. Anything short of this would not satisfy him.

His family thought his obsession would be short-lived, so you can imagine their shock when he told them he was going to move overseas because a needy area of Asia had captured his heart. Most people thought he was throwing his connections and potential out the door. Trading his family fortune for hardship in a Third World country was an entirely different journey than his family and most of their friends had taken.

For the next fifty years, Edward lived a life of purpose and generosity that revolutionized the lives of millions of young people. His passion was to decrease poverty and help people achieve their full potential by discovering God's plan for their lives. He started a school to train young men in how to begin small businesses and make decisions for their businesses and lives based upon the principles of praying, giving, and mentoring. When his students began to implement these principles into daily practice, God blessed. After attending the school, low-class and poorly paid day laborers were able to start businesses of their own and earn money to meet their needs. As soon as a businessman began to make money, Edward encouraged him to give a portion of it away to those less fortunate. Generosity fueled generosity. The students' businesses began growing beyond explanation. In turn, Edward agreed to mentor and train each of his young pupils if and only if each agreed to begin mentoring someone he knew. Edward was multiplying his reach exponentially.

Generosity saved him from living only for himself. His sacrificial choices inspired the choices of millions. His plan was simple: harness all his energy into a few people, spend everything to help them succeed in every area of their lives, coach them until they could help someone else do the same, and believe they would go further than him and serve them until they do. The first group of men he mentored transformed the lives of a few hundred people, but that was only the beginning. The next group connected to thousands of people, and the next group with millions. Throughout his life, Edward hid from notoriety, quietly funneling millions of dollars into the success of others. When you're willing to dispense love this way, there will be no shortage of people needing it. There also will be no shortage from God in giving it.

By the end of Edward's life, he had very few personal possessions of his own. There was not much inheritance to divide between family members. It had all been spent, used, and given to help young men know God and teach them business skills to improve their stations in life. Today a generation of entrepreneurs exists in Asia who got out of poverty because of one man's decision to reflect the image of God to those in need.

HOW GENEROSITY COMPLETES OUR STORIES

Generosity changes our focus from the past to the future and from ourselves to others. Generosity pushes us to meet new people who we are called to help. Actually, these people are an essential part of God's rewriting our own stories. Their stories are incomplete without our involvement, and our stories are unfinished without their need. Generosity completes both parties. The receiver gets his or her needs met; the giver moves that much closer to achieving God's design.

When we understand that others need our generous words of affirmation, pats on the back, sacrifices of love, and unexpected celebrations, we become aware of how strategic our lives really are. When we lift others up, serve people in need, and look for new ways to give, we are actually becoming what God intended for us, and the recipient is as well.

When we are openhanded with our time, money, and possessions, God rewards us with blessings to share. With the overage of God's graciousness, we are able to care for and help those in need. When God orchestrates the generosity, the gift is exactly what is needed to move the recipient's story forward. The greatest reward anyone can have is to help someone else rebuild his or her story. What most of us don't fully realize is that when we give to others, it is God Himself that gives back to us. Our generosity moves God's heart. When we live for something beyond ourselves, we are rewarded. As we give, God gives back to us. In fact, He gives according to how we give. The amazing thing is that God uses the size of our giving as the pattern or mold for His giving to us. *Give, and it will be given to you. . . . With the same measure that you use, it will be measured back to you.*[13]

Lorena and Teresa will tell you that one of the greatest days in their lives was when a need, a gift, and the blessings of God all came together. Teresa and her family had started attending a fast-growing church. As part of a spiritual-growth campaign at the church, she was reading a one-year Bible. One day while reading her Bible, she had a deep sense that she should do something for the pastor and his family. This was the first time she had read the Scriptures and felt as though God were speaking directly to her to do something. She couldn't shake the idea that specifically she was supposed to provide groceries to her pastor's family. She and her husband talked about this new idea, and, along with their daughter, decided they would respond in obedience.

She found Lorena, the pastor's wife, and began making small talk. Lorena could tell by the look on Teresa's face that she was there for more than small talk. Finally, Teresa blurted out, "I don't know why, but I feel like I am supposed to ask you if you have food." Lorena's heart stopped as she choked back the tears. Days earlier, she and her husband were forced to make a difficult choice: either pay for some outreach events for the church plant or pay their own salary. Their decision left little food in the pantry.

When Lorena and her husband got to Teresa's house, Teresa asked them to back their car into the garage. Lorena thought it an odd request, as she was expecting only a few bags of groceries. She said to her husband, "I think you are okay parked here. I'll just run in and get the groceries." But Teresa insisted that they back their car into the garage. When they did, Teresa opened up an upright freezer. It was packed with groceries. Because Teresa traveled for work, she used a delivery service that brought food each month, whether it was needed or not. Over time, the amount of food snowballed into a completely packed freezer. She unloaded the freezer's entire contents into Lorena's car. Teresa had given them six months' worth of groceries!

This is the rewrite: As Lorena and her family sacrificially gave in order to support the growth of a brand-new church, God sent a brand-new believer to meet the needs of Lorena's family. Lorena needed food, and Teresa needed to be in a position of being generous. They needed each other. Both their stories were incomplete without the other. Teresa had no idea about their need, but God did. This was the jump start to her understanding that God wanted to continue speaking to her through the Scriptures. Within weeks of this act of kindness, Teresa received a promotion within her company. The two events became forever linked in her mind. God was taking both the giver and the recipient into a new understanding of how He completes our stories when we are willing to give.

Being generous takes our stories in directions different than we would ever dream, because when we are generous, God responds to us in the same manner. God's only response to us is as the Ultimate Giver.

REWRITING YOUR STORY THROUGH HUMILITY

The staff meeting had been under way for over an hour and every department head was present. Julian's boss turned to him and barked, "Run and get me a grilled Chick-fil-A sandwich for lunch," as he threw a couple of dollars across the table. The tension in the room was thick, and the stares of his peers were like daggers. Everyone was waiting to see how he would respond. His pride was crushed as he walked out the door for yet another errand. By title, Julian was a head manager at a multimillion-dollar organization, but his boss constantly asked him to run errands such as this one. Worse, the boss took credit for Julian's work.

On the way to the restaurant, Julian thought about all the things he'd done to bail out his boss from mess-up after mess-up. There was the time a consulting firm couldn't figure out how to fix a major problem with a vendor. The issue was big enough to take down the entire company. Singlehandedly, Julian had solved the problem, saving the company millions of dollars and the embarrassment of going belly-up. Within his first two years, he had brought in hundreds of new clients, which translated into hundreds of thousands of dollars' worth of business. He had developed a series of training materials that were to be sold through a major bookstore, yet when he opened up the FedEx package to see the sample copy, he saw that his name had been replaced with his boss's name.

As a result of his boss's mistreatment, anger and resentment were overtaking Julian's life. At his wit's end, he said to me (Bruce), "My life is being stolen from me. Despite all my credentials and experience, I am nothing more than an errand boy. Why is this happening to me?"

"I don't think you are going to like the answer," I replied. So eager to find comfort in any answer, he practically leaped across the table. "What?" he asked.

Taking a long deep breath, I responded, "Humility." My answer was not what he'd hoped to hear. "In many ways, the removal of pride from your life will be far more difficult to deal with than the embarrassment inflicted upon you by your boss," I said. "This week I want you to memorize Philippians 2:3: *Do nothing out of selfish ambition or vain conceit, but in humility consider others better than yourselves.* Each time your boss asks you to do something you feel beneath you, recite this verse. Take every task, no matter how inconsequential, and serve him with your actions and attitude as if he has infinite value. Let's connect over coffee after the holidays to see how it's going."

Weeks later I asked Julian, "How's it going with your boss?" With a huge smile on his face, he said, "The night before Thanksgiving, I was headed to the airport to fly home when my phone rang. It was my boss. He asked me to come back to the office to fix an emergency issue in another department."

The first thought that popped into my mind was, *Boy, his boss does have it out for him!* Not wanting to verbalize that,

I cleared my throat and said something more pastoral: "What did you do?"

Julian said, "I did what Philippians 2:3 told me to do. I thanked God for the opportunity to serve my boss. I am beginning to see each demeaning task and delay as an opportunity to thank God for the pain, the people, and even for the plans that I don't understand. It took me hours to figure out the mess. I was able to, but I missed my flight home."

I was stunned. Would I have been humble enough to work through a holiday? Then my curiosity got the better of me. "Why are you smiling about this?" I asked. Julian didn't even miss a beat. "My pride is always a bigger deal than I want to admit. Within me there is arrogance and a constant battle to prove that I am right. God is in the process of exchanging my pride for humility."

I tried to say something profound, and Julian interrupted, saying, "You haven't even heard the best part yet!" By now I was on the edge of my seat. "Yesterday, while standing in line for my boss's dry cleaning, I ran into a buddy I had not seen in years. He invited me to coffee, and within an hour he offered me a job that was beyond my wildest dreams. The offer will double my salary and utilize my gifts to their fullest. It was at the dry cleaners that God opened up the door to give me something I could have never pulled off myself. While my life seemed to be on hold, God was cultivating humility in my life through my boss's demands. Performing yet another humbling task put me in the very place for God to give me something better than I could imagine."

What God did for Julian is exactly what He wants to do for the rest of us. Most of us have a hard time imagining that we could find fulfillment and satisfaction in the midst of humbling experiences, so we run from them. In reality, God often uses different humbling experiences—obscurity, delays, and small tasks performed outside the limelight—to shape our stories in ways we never foresee. Humility positions us to trust in God rather than in our own abilities and plans. It removes self and entrusts our future into His hands. It refocuses our attention onto God's plans.

You might think your story is of no value because most of the assignments that come your way seem insignificant and unimportant. Or maybe your story just seems stuck. But the truth is, you might be in the best place you could ever be. Most people's stories are not nicely packaged with a matching bow on top. In fact, most start small and have interruptions, ups and downs, and a few cliff-hangers along the way. That was certainly the case with David, the shepherd boy.

OBSCURITY: WHEN LIFE SEEMS TO PASS YOU BY

From all outward appearances, David had a story that was going nowhere. He was the eighth son born into a busy family of all boys. While his brothers went off to fight in a war, David had to stay home and tend smelly sheep. Not exactly a heroic or exciting profession. The dreams and plans he may have had for his life were drowned out by the sounds of sheep. But God had a much greater story in mind for this undervalued shepherd boy.

When God told the Old Testament prophet Samuel to anoint the next king of Israel, Samuel went to the home of Jesse, David's father, expecting God to make one of David's brothers king. Jesse called seven of his eight sons into the house to prepare for the anointing ceremony. What a tremendous honor! One by one Samuel surveyed the young men. One by one Samuel, under

God's counsel, ruled each one out. Then Samuel asked Jesse, *Are all the young men here?*[1]

So unimportant did David appear that even his own father didn't bother to call him into the house for the ceremony. In the fields watching sheep, David had no idea what was happening. His father's response to the prophet seems dismissive: *There remains yet the youngest, and there he is, keeping the sheep.*[2] Jesse implied that David was too young and in far too lowly a position to be a candidate for the highest position in the kingdom.

When David was called from the field, he was plucked from obscurity and placed before Samuel. Immediately, the Lord said, *This is the one!*[3] Can you imagine the scene? The seven older brothers had the opportunity to clean up for the ceremony and were standing in their best clothes, expecting that one of them would be anointed. Instead, they watch as the young David, dirty from being in the pastures, was anointed as the next king of Israel.

God's divine anointing found David despite his obscurity. God is always working behind the scenes to bring about His purposes.[4] The beginning of David's training for his future role as king began in one of the lowliest professions of his day. The pasture was no obstacle for God; He used it to prepare David for the assignment for which he was created.

God delights in using the least-expected person for His purposes. *The LORD does not see as man sees; for man looks at the outward appearance, but the LORD looks at the heart.*[5] How others view us makes no difference in God's eyes. You might not be the smartest, strongest, or most athletic, but God sees you differently. He is not concerned with your position, title, or appearance. "Obscurity is not a handicap to greatness";[6] in fact, it is the starting point!

Rarely does God give people a huge assignment without first

refining their character; He wants our character to match the
tasks He has created for us. We all know people who received a
promotion and then their character could not sustain their
position. Pride set in and ruined their personality and attitude.
God resists the proud, but gives grace to the humble.[7] God wants to
remove pride from our lives and replace it with humility. To do
this, He shapes our character outside the limelight and away from
the praise and accolades of others. If we are in the background,
God has room to develop our character in order to more accu-
rately reflect His image.

I (Heather) know this firsthand. At one point in our ministry,
I asked Bruce how I could be the most useful to him. Because I
had a seminary degree and had been in full-time ministry prior to
our marriage, I thought he might ask me to oversee a large ministry area or create a women's ministry. His response was not what
I had hoped to hear. He asked me to clean the church every week
before Sunday services, especially the bathrooms! To add insult to
injury, the building we were meeting in at the time was not up to
code, and the septic tanks regularly (and I stress *regularly*) got
backed up and flooded the restroom floors. He knew that if young
families walked onto a sewage-soaked restroom, the chances of
them returning to church were slim.

I didn't like holding the toilet bowl brush in my hand. I
thought the toilet bowl brush would prevent me from something
big. How was I to ever be the well-known pastor's wife with a
thriving ministry? How would my years of ministry experience
ever be used to their fullest inside a closet full of cleaning supplies?
More than once I asked God why I had to be the one cleaning
toilets. More than once I heard Him say, "You are exactly where I
want you," which was behind the scenes, in the background, far,
far away from the spotlight.

It was months before I could clean toilets and be happy about it. Ultimately, I wasn't doing it for Bruce or even for the guests at church. I was cleaning for God. *Whatever you do, work at it with all your heart, as working for the Lord, not for men, since you know that you will receive an inheritance from the Lord as a reward. It is the Lord Christ you are serving.*[8] The moment I invited God to join me in my obscurity, my attitude changed.

God worked on my heart because I invited Him to join me behind the scenes. As I cleaned, I also prayed. I thanked God for the opportunity to clean. I prayed for the men and women who would walk through the doors of the church. I prayed that their hearts and lives would be changed by God's saving grace. Each week in the church bathrooms, I had my own personal prayer service. God showed up for my benefit. With no one present except God and me, it was a holy moment each week. In an odd way, I looked forward to spending that time with God. It became less about the task itself and more about my time with Him. Inviting Him into my obscurity not only changed my perspective but also my feelings about the situation. When God enters into the ordinary details of our lives with all His power, might, and glory, something extraordinary happens. The moment becomes holy and life defining.

Story Builders

- Read about David's story in 1 Samuel 16:1-13. What about David's story resonates with you?
- What about your talents, background, or strength have others overlooked?

- What has God used to remove pride and build up humility in your life?
- Read Proverbs 11:2 and 18:12 to see what God says about pride and humility. Choose one of these to memorize and recite the next time you feel as if your pride is getting the better of you.

David's story also illustrates how God uses delays to bring out His story in our lives.

DELAYS: GIVE IT UP!

When God brings delays into our lives, He is asking, "Will you trust Me rather than yourself?" So often we think that God is saying no to something in our lives when it doesn't happen in the timing we expect, but this isn't necessarily the case. Delays can serve a bigger purpose. They can give us the opportunity to lay aside our own plans and perspective and to trust that God is in charge and knows what He is doing. Delays provide us with the opportunity to put aside our pride and self-aggrandizement in order to showcase God.

This was true for David. You might assume that after he was anointed the next king of Israel, he would wear priceless robes, eat fine foods, and have servants at his beck and call. But that was not to be. He experienced a huge delay before ever sitting on the throne as king. First, he became Saul's servant. He was recruited to play the harp and sing when Saul had one of his depressing mood swings. David humbly trusted in God's timing. He was more concerned for Saul's emotional well-being than his own political status. He put Saul's needs above his own. To top it off, when Saul was in a good mood and didn't need David's services, where do you think David was? *David occasionally went and returned from Saul to feed his father's sheep at Bethlehem.*[9] That's right, David was still tending the sheep!

In the midst of this delay, David waited for God to work and gave up what was rightly his. He could have claimed the king's crown and luxurious robes as his own. Instead, he clothed himself in humility by putting his shepherd's clothes back on.

The delay gave David the opportunity to mirror God. There is no quality more godlike than humility in the face of delays.

> *In humility consider others better than yourselves. Each of you should look not only to your own interests, but also to the interests of others.*
> *Your attitude should be the same as that of Christ Jesus:*
>
> *Who, being in very nature God,*
> *did not consider equality with God something to be grasped,*
> *but made himself nothing,*
> *taking the very nature of a servant,*
> *being made in human likeness.*
> *And being found in appearance as a man,*
> *he humbled himself*
> *and became obedient to death—even death on a cross!*[10]

Delays present us with the opportunity to humbly trust God and wait for His plan to unfold. Heather and I were reminded of this on a trip we took when she was seven months pregnant with our daughter. We had decided to take a vacation while she could still fly, and I wanted to show Heather Boston, one of my favorite cities. Our first day there, we ate at one of the oldest restaurants in the city. I ordered the fish cakes. Three bites in, I swallowed bone slivers from the fish. I went to the bathroom; meanwhile, Heather remained at our table.

After fifteen minutes, she came to check on me. I was hunched over the bathroom sink, trying to cough up the fish bones, and the restaurant's doorman had the restroom door propped opened for all to see. The bones were deeply lodged in my throat, so the only option was to call 911. The EMTs finally arrived and loaded us into the ambulance. With sirens blaring, they raced to the hospital. Two doctors, five nurses, and four hours later, all the bones were removed.

This was a major setback on our quick two-day trip to Boston. I was more than upset. It was supposed to be the perfect day planned just for Heather. I bought tickets ahead of time for a tour of the city, picked out the best restaurant, and planned a shopping trip for her, and now my pregnant wife was taking care of me. The day was ruined.

We got into our rental car, determined to carry on with the vacation. Not wanting the entire day to be wasted, I pulled the car over for an unscheduled stop to show Heather one of my favorite city parks. As we were pulling in, three black SUVs with tinted windows drove past us. Men with earpieces stepped out of two of the cars and started canvassing the area. Out of curiosity, I drove a little closer. Just then, the president of the United States stepped out of the third SUV! I put the car in park and shouted, "Heather, get out of the car! We are going to meet the president." We were close enough to see the fierce looks on the faces of the Secret Service.

"Bruce," she said, "they don't look too happy that we are here. I am seven months pregnant and don't feel like getting shot today!"

To which I replied, "Exactly. They won't shoot a pregnant lady."

We got out of our car to find the president and his wife ordering ice cream from a local vendor. We shook the president's hand and had a casual five-minute conversation with him! Had we not experienced the delay with fish bones, we never would have been in the position to meet the president. The pain of the pause positioned us for an opportunity of a lifetime!

As we drove off, I began to think about delays and how God might be using them to orchestrate His purposes for our lives. I thought to myself, *Is there any area of my life that I'm trying to move forward in that God may be delaying?* My mind raced to a building we tried to lease on several occasions for our growing church. It was the only building in our area for lease, and it was right next to our church property. It would have allowed us to expand by another one hundred people. Suddenly, I was jolted with the fact that I had tried to push the lease through several times and nothing ever happened. The owner needed the rental money, but my idea was met with one delay after another. The delays frustrated me because I was desperate to make room for new families. I decided to embrace the delays and not push any further. It was a humbling experience to know that I had no other option than to trust God for future developments. I was learning that humility was about trusting in God's plans versus trying to push through my own. Maybe God was rearranging things for a better story.

Weeks later, that delay enabled our church to experience God's plan, which went far beyond reaching another one hundred people. His plan was to reach another thousand people with the hope and love of Jesus through a partnership with another church. Had I arrogantly pushed through with my plans, I never would have been open to partnering with others. That's how God works. When we bring delays to God and trust Him to work out His plan for our lives through those delays, our trusting and humble attitudes mirror Christ's humility to the world and open the door for God to give us better stories than we would have settled for.

~~Story~~ Builders

- Read 1 Samuel 16:14-22. What about David's delay between being crowned king and actually ascending to the throne resonates with you?
- Have you ever felt that your life was "on hold"? If so, what were the circumstances?
- How did God use the delay for your benefit (teach you something about yourself or God, root out pride and cultivate humility)?
- Delays require us to wait on God. Read Psalm 5:3 and 37:7. Choose one to commit to memory and recite every time you feel the need to rush ahead of Him.

SMALL IS THE NEW BIG

God uses small tasks to give us an opportunity to learn humility and position us for something bigger. This too was part of David's story. After he returned home to watch the family's sheep, his father was worried about David's older brothers on the battlefield and asked David to take food to them. Little did David know that God had a momentous purpose for having him do this seemingly menial task. Because David accepted the job, he was put in the position of being able to bring about an extraordinary defeat of Goliath, the nation's top enemy.

His errand became a window of opportunity to be at the right place at the right time and, more important, be the right person to take the giant down.

Jesse could have chosen any of his four other sons or numerous servants to carry the meal to his sons on the battle-field, yet he chose David. Why? In his perception, David was the youngest and the least skilled. He was good for being an errand boy. David willingly and humbly accepted the assignment. No complaining, no eye rolling.

With baskets of food in hand, David arrived just as Goliath was taunting Israel's army. David overheard the men talking about the giant and saw their fear. He asked, *What shall be done for the man who kills this Philistine and takes away the reproach from Israel? For who is this uncircumcised Philistine, that he should defy the armies of the living God?*[11] David's errand placed him directly in front of a giant named Goliath, who stood nine feet tall and wore a bronze helmet and armor. What a menacing figure for a young shepherd to confront!

Saul could not understand David's boldness. Because Goliath was an experienced soldier, David seemed a foolish challenger for the ultimate fighting champion.

> *But David said to Saul, "Your servant has been keeping his father's sheep. When a lion or a bear came and carried off a sheep from the flock, I went after it, struck it and rescued the sheep from its mouth. When it turned on me, I seized it by its hair, struck it and killed it. Your servant has killed both the lion and the bear; this uncircumcised Philistine will be like one of them, because he has defied the armies of the living God. The LORD who delivered me from the paw of the lion and the paw of the bear will deliver me from the hand of this Philistine."*[12]

The daily responsibilities that David fulfilled as a common shepherd were the building blocks for a larger assignment: the defeat of Goliath. *Whoever can be trusted with very little can also be trusted with much.*[13]

As he confronted Goliath, the errand boy was transformed into a warrior:

> *You come against me with sword and spear and javelin, but I come against you in the name of the LORD Almighty, the God of the armies of Israel, whom you have defied. . . . All those gathered here will know that it is not by sword or spear that the LORD saves; for the battle is the LORD's, and he will give all of you into our hands.*[14]

This was David's defining moment. He was about to become a giant killer and be catapulted into national stardom.

> *David put his hand in his bag and took out a stone; and he slung it and struck the Philistine in his forehead, so that the stone sank into his forehead, and he fell on his face to the earth. So David prevailed over the Philistine with a sling and a stone, and struck the Philistine and killed him. . . . And when the Philistines saw that their champion was dead, they fled.*[15]

One shepherd boy on a simple errand used one smooth stone to defeat an entire nation. *Clothe yourselves, all of you, with humility toward one another. . . . Humble yourselves, therefore, under the mighty hand of God so that at the proper time he may exalt you.*[16] Because David chose humility, God exalted him. When he took the humble assignment from his father, God honored him. Prior to this small task of bringing food to his brothers, no one knew David, but by the time Goliath hit the ground, David was a household name. When we trust God by taking on small tasks that seem beneath us, it opens the door for God to exalt us in ways we never could have manufactured on our own. This is how humility works. It places us in a position to trust in God only, and it rewrites our stories where only God can get the credit.

~~Story~~ Builders

- Read 1 Samuel 17:14-51 to experience David's stunning defeat of Goliath.
- What small tasks have you been currently assigned? Are you performing them to the best of your ability? Are you reflecting humility as you perform the small assignments?
- How might God use small tasks to create an even better story for you?
- God promises to reward your humility. Check out 1 Peter 5:6.

REWRITING YOUR STORY THROUGH SUFFERING

As soon as Kelly stepped into my office at the church, I could tell something was wrong. The large black sunglasses were an attempt to hide her bloodshot and swollen eyes, but they failed to mask the pain written all over her face. Her husband, Javier, had come with her. Their teenage daughter was making a string of disastrous choices. Once the good girl, she rejected almost overnight all the values and self-respect her parents had tried to instill in her. She had all the wrong friends and dated a string of druggies and dropouts. On more than one occasion, Javier rode around town in search of his daughter because she did not come home at curfew. Kelly and Javier were living a nightmare that was made all the more painful as they watched their friends' children make the honor roll and become star athletes. This was not anywhere near the life plans and dreams they had for their daughter. Then came the unplanned pregnancy and a deadbeat boyfriend; they were now in the exhausting world of raising both their daughter and a beautiful new granddaughter. They were entangled in a world of diapers and personality conflicts.

Their frustration had hit a whole new level. I asked them, "What if you could go back and reverse your story and everything that has happened to your daughter? There would be no unplanned pregnancy, no painful rejection from the baby's father, no personality conflicts, and less financial strain."

For the first time since Kelly entered my office, her facial expressions indicated relief. "I would love that!" she said quickly.

I went on to say, "But that would also mean there is no little girl to smile at you when you come in from a long day, no tiny hugs, no kisses, and no dreams for her little life."

At that moment, Kelly and Javier realized the great joy that had come out of their pain. To give up the pain also meant giving up the blessing. That is simply how most of life is. Through sorrow, God births new stories, better than the ones we could have made up on our own.

Suffering rewrote Kelly and Javier's story, causing them to reflect Christ's character in a greater way. *This High Priest of ours understands our weaknesses, for he faced all of the same testings we do, yet he did not sin.*[1] Kelly and Javier are now more like Him because they are empathetic to others in crises. Because Christ identifies with us and shows compassion in the midst of our suffering, we too can identify with others who are experiencing painful lives.

Today, Kelly and Javier have incredible opportunities to speak into the lives of parents dealing with teen pregnancies. They counsel and pray with moms and dads who see only shattered dreams. Their story of helping raise a granddaughter and the joy she brings to their lives brings hope to others facing similar circumstances.

Suffering like this causes enormous pain and unexpected loss. When deep pain enters our lives, bitterness befriends us quickly and fear tries to drown us. If we listen to these opponents, we will never see that suffering can actually be what God uses to exchange our stories for a greater story.

Painful experiences come in various forms: a lie that bankrupts a business, an affair that sabotages a marriage, a chronic illness, a broken engagement, a financial meltdown of a family. And although not everyone has experienced the same events in life, most of us have experienced a level of pain that seems unbearable. When suffering interrupts our lives and shatters everything of value, we feel that we have lost all chance at happiness. Our dreams and goals have been derailed. However, suffering and pain don't have to be dead ends. If we allow Him to, God can heal our suffering and use the painful experiences to direct us and rewrite our stories into new stories. Suffering can showcase God's glory and reveal a level of grace we never would have seen had our lives been left untouched.

GOD BRINGS BEAUTY OUT OF OUR SUFFERING

Every painful experience has with it the assurance that God is creating something out of the loss. He rewrites our story by bringing something good out of our pain. "We think broken things are a loss, but God turns them into gain. In nature broken things are cast aside; but in grace, God will never use a man until he is broken."[2]

With each moment that we suffer, God brings us gifts that change our perspective and allow other people to see His grace in our lives. Let's take a look at the different gifts suffering brings.

The Gift of God's Constant Presence
When we go through a crisis, we are not left to suffer alone. *God is our refuge and strength, always ready to help in times of trouble.*[3]

"We are never deserted when we encounter such ordeals, but we are able to turn to our unfailing friend of grace and solicit help in time of need."[4]

The Gift of God's Favor and Protection

When people go through times of great hurt, God's heart goes out to them. His favor follows the brokenhearted, as does His protection. *The sacrifices of God are a broken spirit, a broken and a contrite heart—these, O God, You will not despise.*[5] *The LORD is near to the brokenhearted and saves those who are crushed in spirit.*[6]

The Gift of His Perspective

Brokenness helps us see the needs of others that we were blind to before. Brokenness allows us to see as God sees.

> *Fierce troubles came down on the people of those churches, pushing them to the very limit. The trial exposed their true colors: They were incredibly happy, though desperately poor. The pressure triggered something totally unexpected: an outpouring of pure and generous gifts. I was there and saw it for myself. They gave offerings of whatever they could—far more than they could afford!—pleading for the privilege of helping out in the relief of poor Christians.*[7]

The Gift of Healing

God lovingly places bandages on the deepest wounds of our hearts. *He heals the brokenhearted and binds up their wounds.*[8]

The Gift of Safety, Rest, and Comfort

God also gifts us with safety, rest, and comfort. *He is my loving God and my fortress, my stronghold and my deliverer, my shield, in whom I take refuge.*[9] He offers us a safety net in the midst of turmoil. Some wounds are so deep that the words of a friend won't heal them, nor can the words of a professional counselor fix them. In those deep, dark places of life, God is our deliverer. We find safety and protection in Him. *I cried out to You, O LORD: I said, "You are my refuge, my portion in the land of the living."*[10]

God's care for creation is infinite, and the depth of His love for us unsearchable. Tragedy prepares our hearts and minds to receive the deepest comfort and grace God has to offer. *Praise be to the God and Father of our Lord Jesus Christ, the Father of compassion and the God of all comfort. . . . For just as the sufferings of Christ flow over into our lives, so also through Christ our comfort overflows.*[11] There is no problem we go through that God's consolation can't reach; He is the God of all comfort. He has everything we need. Probably the best news of all is that God matches His level of grace and comfort according to the level of our pain. In the most agonizing trials of life, God's comfort toward us abounds. *Surely goodness and mercy shall follow me all the days of my life.*[12] His mercy and grace chase after us.

The Gift of the Opportunity to Know the Depth of God's Power

If life were without pain, we would never be able to mine the depths of God's care for us. Without sickness, we would need no Healer. Without anxiety and fear, we would have no need for a safe place to rest our minds and hearts. Without death and despair, we would have no need for comfort. Our afflictions leave room for God to show up with all the abundant resources of His power and glory and to enter into the deepest hurts of life. Our suffering as well as God's character are on display, side by side, to a broken world. God's glory shines at its brightest in the midst of our greatest difficulties. In our weakness, God's strength and glory are most visible.

We see this in the Bible story of the man who was blind from birth. In the ancient world, blindness was a disability that could not be overcome. Blindness and other conditions left a person with only one career path, so this man sat year after year on the side of a dirt road as a beggar. Each day started and ended the same. The best he could hope for was a morsel of food or some small coins dropped into his cup. He heard thousands of people walk past him, and most never even acknowledged him. Beyond needing food and money, what this blind man was desperate for was grace. He was living each day without hope: no hope of a cure, no hope of a job, and no hope of finding a meaningful place in society. Blind he was born, and a beggar he would die.

Then one day, a day that started out as another day without hope, the beggar encountered the one Person who could use his suffering to turn his story into something he had long ago stopped even dreaming about. The disciples, who traveled with Jesus, saw the blind beggar. Within earshot of the beggar, they asked Jesus, *Who sinned, this man or his parents, that he was born blind?*[13] Jesus, full of compassion and hope, answered, *Neither this man nor his parents sinned . . . but this happened so that the work of God might be displayed in his life.*[14] Jesus passed by, as had thousands of others, but He did what no other person could do: He healed the man.[15]

God's healing power was on display because the man's eyes were broken. For the first time in his life, he was able to feast on things not seen before: his parents, his surroundings, and the people who passed him by day after day. The whole town knew that the man was born without sight, and, even more important, the whole town now knew the power of Jesus. Suddenly, the man, his parents, townspeople, and the religious leaders were swept up in debate about Jesus' healing power. Undeniably, a blind man could now see.

When God shows up in the midst of your pain and difficulty, it puts the world on notice. Your weakness only causes God's glory and power to shine even brighter. In the midst of your most painful memory, toxic relationship, or brutal intrusion, God wants His glory to be on display for a messed-up world.

"To us, broken things are tragedies but to God they are opportunities to be used for His glory."[16] God's perspective is that only broken things are ready for His grace; only broken things are available to be recaptured for His purpose. Had the formerly blind man been able to see from birth, he would have had a different story. He would likely have apprenticed in his dad's business. He would have been married, and he would have been in the temple worshipping on his own. He would not have been sitting on a dusty road the day Jesus walked by. He might never have gotten a one-on-one appointment with the Son of God! He never would have received a miracle, because there is no need of a miracle when nothing is broken. The blind man would never have been the vehicle of God's glory.

People followed Jesus from town to town because they were in awe of His power. To the religious elite, the hodgepodge of followers must have looked like a circus sideshow of odd, unusual, and pathetic individuals following a pied piper. The lame, blind, sick, and demon-possessed clamored for Jesus' attention. Traveling from far and wide to stand before the One they had heard could heal their afflictions, the needy begged for grace and mercy. He healed them all. He *forgives all your sins and heals all your diseases*.[17] "Trials touch the most vital interests of our lives, but at the same time they bring vividly to light the holy presence of the Healer and the assurance of His help."[18]

Jesus does healing work that no physician is capable of. He takes on cases no one else can take on. No medicine in the world can be prescribed to heal a broken heart. But in light of eternity, when the human heart is crushed, suffering cannot defeat us. The work of Jesus Christ on the cross allows us to partake in the ultimate victory over the brokenness in our lives: *Death has been swallowed up in victory. Where, O death, is your victory? Where, O death, is your sting?*[19]

In every painful experience we have, God is creating something beautiful that will rewrite our story. The event may not be good, but God will make sure that He works it out for our ultimate good. *And we know that all things work together for good to those who love God, to those who are the called according to His purpose.*[20]

Over time, God can use your suffering to move your story to a different place. He doesn't want your pain to turn you into a victim. He has so much more in mind for you, and He offers you the power to live the story He has designed for you.

~~Story~~ Builders

- Read Romans 8:28. This verse promises that God uses all circumstances in our lives for our good. What difficulties are you experiencing right now? How might God be using them for your good? Commit this verse to memory. This is a great verse to recite when you are experiencing difficulty and are tempted to think God has forgotten you.
- What gifts have you experienced from suffering? How has suffering allowed you to reflect God's image to a broken world?

- Log on to www.RewriteMyStory.com and tell us how God has brought you through a difficult situation. Your story can bring hope to thousands of others going through similar circumstances.

YOUR STORY IS JUST BEGINNING

When suffering interrupts our lives, God's attention is focused on us and He brings His total might and glory to work on our behalf. We're unaware of all He's doing behind the scenes to turn around our stories.

"If you are being broken, God is working with you. He is making something that will someday astound you with its wisdom and beauty."[21] You need to know that your story is not over.

Just ask Dan and Casey. They dreamed of having a beautiful baby to love and raise as their own. From the beginning of her pregnancy, Casey had one prayer: that God would use her baby to help make her into the woman God designed her to be.

Casey loved photography and planned to catch every special moment of her child's life on film: the first baby step to the steps across a graduation stage, to the steps down the church aisle at a wedding. Dreaming and planning built the excitement and anticipation for these first-time parents.

With each sonogram, the baby moved and the heartbeat was strong. Casey's heart swelled with the pride and love she felt for her baby. Things seemed to be going along just fine, with the exception that they could not discover the sex of the baby. During the twenty-eighth week of her pregnancy, they decided to go to a 3D ultrasound facility for one more try.

The next morning, the doctor called and shared the results of the ultrasound. Forever embedded in Casey's mind were the words "Your baby has a condition where the organs grow outside the body and possibly a chromosomal disorder. This is almost always fatal to the baby."

What cruel words for a first-time mom to hear. Months later, Casey gave birth to a beautiful baby boy named Asher. The best surgeons, nurses, and neonatal specialists were in the room waiting for his arrival, but they were unable to keep him alive.

Casey left the hospital that day with empty arms. When friends stopped by with meals, there was no baby to proudly show off. She would never get to see Asher's smile or hear his laugh. There would be no birthday parties to plan and no soccer games to attend. Instead, the one thing Casey did get to plan was the funeral of her tiny son.

Suffering showed Dan and Casey they ultimately would have to be sustained by God alone. There was no human intervention that could make the loss go away. When our response to suffering brings us to a place of dependence on God alone, He responds to us in grace. Casey prayed this daily prayer:

God please heal my baby completely.
But if not, please let my baby live for a while so we can know him.
But if not, please let my baby live for a few hours so we can hold and kiss him.
But if not, please let my baby live till it's born.
But if not, please let my baby live through tomorrow.
But if not, hold me tightly so I can live through tomorrow!

The end of Casey's prayer conveys how, ultimately, God was going to have to hold and sustain her.

God infused His comfort and grace into Dan and Casey. He took their sorrow and turned it into something beautiful, and today theirs is a home full of love, laughter, and the pitter patter of little feet. Just months after the loss of their son, they began praying about adoption. On November 29, they received a packet of information from an adoption agency. Their plan was to fill out the paperwork, continue to pray, and wait for a baby.

Because God is always working things for our good, He was about to pour out His grace on Dan and Casey. The telephone rang. Someone from the agency was calling. Then came the words that made Casey's heart leap: "There is a woman who wants to put her baby up for adoption and hasn't found a family for her yet. She is due December 6. She wants a two-parent home and a Christian family for the baby within her. Would you be interested in adopting her?" It was as though God were saying, "Here is something beautiful in the midst of your pain!" *How great is the goodness you have stored up for those who fear you. You lavish it on those who come to you for protection, blessing them before the watching world.*[22] God knew there was a baby who needed a pair of loving arms to hold her, and He knew there was a mother with empty arms who needed a baby to love. Seven days later, God's glory and grace were on display as Casey and Dan held their little girl.

~~Story~~ Builders

- Second Corinthians 1:3-7 is a wonderful reminder that God is our Comforter when we go through painful experiences. What trials have you faced in the past? How has God shown comfort to you?
- What are the biggest lessons you have learned from suffering?

- Are you going through a painful experience now? Remember, the work of Jesus Christ on the cross makes Him able to identify with all your suffering. Read and meditate on Hebrews 4:15-16. How does this encourage you in the midst of pain?
- What is the basis of our strength? Check out 2 Corinthians 12:8-10; 1 Peter 5:9-11; Psalm 119:73-80.

HEROES NEEDED!

People who overcome adversity inspire us and give us hope. We want to be like them. That's why when the Olympics are on, we sit glued to the TV. There is just something inspiring about disciplined athletes who push their aching muscles past the point of what seems humanly possible. We root for athletes who show up with a limp or torn muscle for the event they have trained for their whole lives. We cheer for these athletes because something within us just wants so badly for the underdog to win.

Most of us will never be Olympic athletes; however, at some point in life we will be the underdog. With the odds stacked against us, we ask ourselves, *Will adversity take us down? Will the betrayal cause us to recoil in pain? Will the divorce cause us to never trust again? Will the long-term illness cause us to give up?*

When we overcome the odds, it provides inspiration and hope for others struggling in a similar way. In fact, the world needs us to overcome our affliction because the world is full of people who have given up. Our suffering can help rewrite the story of others. *He comforts us in all our troubles so that we can comfort others. When they are troubled, we will be able to give them the same comfort God has given us.*[23] God's comfort to us is ultimately a gift given with the responsibility to pass it on to others in need. Our lives are meant to be stories that represent God to a broken world. "He intends that these trials of our faith should turn to testimonies, so that we are able to recount our experiences of deliverance in telling others of the riches of His character especially in times of distress."[24] God comforts us so that our afflictions become testimonies by which to help others. When we comfort others, we bear the image of God as His representatives of comfort.

We all have friends, family, coworkers, and children desperate for us to step up and learn the faith-building lessons that come only through adversity. Until we know heartache, we never have reason to throw ourselves at the mercy of God. Until we have pain, we cannot inspire others to overcome adversity and suffering.

How easy it is to think of our suffering as pointless! But just because we don't like it or don't understand it doesn't mean it is useless. There will be a day when God *will wipe every tear from their eyes, and there will be no more death or sorrow or crying or pain.*[25] Until that day comes, this broken world needs heroes. This world needs hope and inspiration found in men and women who endure hardship and emerge victoriously. Let us tell you the story of two such heroes, Lisa and Angie.

Lisa was from a broken home, the type where alcohol and drug abuse was commonplace. Growing up, she was often cursed at and told such things as, "I wish you were never born!" The yelling was bad enough, but the blows to her head were demoralizing. Her parents, while married, openly brought other lovers into the home. Much of her early childhood was spent completely alone, without any adult supervision. When she did have babysitters, they hurt her as much as the parents who were supposed to be raising her. Things were not just messed up in Lisa's home; they were hopelessly, desperately wrong. By the time she was twelve, Lisa was walking to the store to buy her own groceries. She was doing her laundry and cooking her own food. She was raising herself. Pain, betrayal, fear, and hurt were the four walls of her cage. She grew up unloved and unable to trust anyone.

Most people would look at Lisa's life and give her little chance of overcoming her past, saying that the odds were stacked against her. Little did Lisa know it, but the chase was on. God was pursuing her, drawing her to Himself. For a year, friends kept inviting Lisa to church. She finally caved at an invitation for a hot-dog supper. A church service followed the dinner, and Lisa listened as the pastor shared how the extravagant love of Jesus Christ led Him to die on the cross for people's sins. This was the kind of love she had longed for. It answered the deepest need of her heart. She desperately wanted to experience what the pastor was talking about. This was the beginning of her rewrite, but there was so much more that was needed to complete her story.

Lisa wrestled with a fear of intimacy and a level of insecurity most people couldn't even imagine. Some days, just meeting a new friend for coffee would terrify her. But God would not leave her hanging. His attention was focused on completing her story and rewriting her past. Lisa was totally dependent on God, and her knees touched the ground several times a day in prayer. With every prayer, she felt the healing of God and a new realization that she was loved unconditionally.

God's healing gave her a new compassion for people and freed her to see deeply into other people's hurts. She could read people who had gone through similar tragedies within seconds of meeting them. When she shared a minute of her own story and how God was transforming her, it would awaken people to talk about things they had buried for years. Her vulnerability about personal struggles, painful events, and the healing that Jesus was doing was the lifeline others were looking for.

When Lisa met Angie for the first time, she wasn't meeting the Angie God designed but the Angie who was formed through the multiple rejections of people. Angie was a teenager who had been abused in multiple foster homes. In each home she was used, and in each home she was discarded. Not one relative invited her in; not one asked her to stay. She grew up thinking she was not valuable enough to keep around. When Lisa asked Angie how she could help, Angie said, "I haven't known anyone for more than a few months. If you want to help me, just be my friend and don't leave."

Lisa says, "A year into our friendship, Angie knew three things about me: that I wasn't going anywhere, that God wasn't going anywhere, and that we both loved her." Lisa's painful days of suffering as a child and her fear of intimacy as an adult were being transformed to healing and inspiration for others who were thirsty for help.

Lisa has stayed put and been a friend to Angie for eight years now. In those years, Angie has tackled some of her own huge issues of forgiveness and dropped some barriers of relationship fear. Angie saw Lisa's story being *Rewritten* and knew that God could change hers as well. Angie told Lisa recently, "I knew that if God could change you, He could change me." Angie needed what we all crave: someone who will walk us through how God can start rewriting our struggles.

The process God uses to rewrite our stories goes way beyond making superficial changes. Suffering and adversity often bring long-lasting changes and bring us back to His original design for us. "It is the purpose of the Lord ultimately to make us like Christ. That means there must be suffering, pain and sorrow in our lives. No believer will ever be like Christ without these afflictions, similar to those which Christ experienced so deeply."[26]

The process of being more like Christ is an ongoing endeavor. *Put on your new nature, and be renewed as you learn to know your Creator and become like him.*[27] As marred image bearers, our natural inclination is to become bitter or to give up in the face of suffering and adversity. Again, we are reminded, *Put off your old self, which is being corrupted by its deceitful desires; to be made new in the attitude of your minds; and to put on the new self, created to be like God in true righteousness and holiness.*[28] The process of transformation takes our tarnished images and renews them day by day so that they better reflect the image of God.

Because God is the Creator of time, He sees beyond the temporal. He looks to the eternal and wants to do something permanent in our lives. *Outwardly we are wasting away, yet inwardly we are being renewed day by day. For our light and momentary troubles are achieving for us an eternal glory that far outweighs them all. So we fix our eyes not on what is seen, but on what is unseen. For what is seen is temporary, but what is unseen is eternal.*[29]

When we see adversity as God's opportunity to fine-tune our stories, we can meet it with joy and expectation. "There are many blessings we will never obtain if we are unwilling to accept and endure suffering."[30] *Dear friends, do not be surprised at the painful trial you are suffering, as though something strange were happening to you. But rejoice that you participate in the sufferings of Christ, so that you may be overjoyed when his glory is revealed.*[31] In fact, God has set aside special rewards for those who overcome suffering. For example:

- **We are co-rulers with Christ.** *If we endure, we shall also reign with Him.*[32]
- **We will receive a special crown.** *Blessed is the man who perseveres under trial, because when he has stood the test, he*

will receive the crown of life that God has promised to those who love him.[33]

- **We are heirs to the riches of heaven.** *For his Spirit joins with our spirit to affirm that we are God's children. And since we are his children, we are his heirs. In fact, together with Christ we are heirs of God's glory. But if we are to share his glory, we must also share his suffering. Yet what we suffer now is nothing compared to the glory he will reveal to us later.*[34]

"It is from suffering that the strongest souls ever known have emerged. The world's greatest display of character is seen in those who exhibit the scars of sorrow."[35] When an Olympic athlete stands to receive the glory of the gold medal, he or she is not standing as the same person who began the discipline of training some ten or fifteen years earlier. That athlete had not known injury or defeat. That athlete had not known the sorrow of being disqualified in a semifinal round. Over the years, the athlete's body has been bruised and battered, and there may have been some broken bones along the way. But all of that combined is what produces the athlete who overcomes adversity to stand proud and tall on the winner's stand. If you took away all the painful moments in the athlete's life, you would most assuredly have to take back the winning medal. Suffering has its rewards.

So it is with our stories. Blessings are born out of tragedy. Behind the scenes and in the places of deepest hurt in your life, God is making you more like His Son and infusing your story with grace.

~~Story~~ Builders

- Who have you seen overcome adversity? What inspires you about them?
- What character qualities exist in your life as a result of suffering? Make a list of some events or qualities that might be missing from your life had you not undergone this difficulty.
- Are there people you know going through a similar experience? If so, God wants to give you an opportunity to reflect His comfort and character to them. How can your story be an inspiration to them? What practical thing can you do to encourage and help them be overcomers?
- Memorize John 16:33. The next time pain and suffering enter your life, recite these verses to remember that because Jesus has overcome, He gives us the ability to be overcomers as well.

STORY KILLERS

When you are living the life God created you to live, expect to encounter story killers, which will try to get you off track. Story killers are things that can stop the transformation process and keep us from living to our full potential. They try to remove God's story from our lives. Story killers are silent and creep up on us. Before we know it, we can be paralyzed by their presence in our lives. Story killers rob us of the blessings God has in store for us and prevent us from being vessels of hope and grace to those in need.

Let's look at two common story killers and how to keep them from destroying the story God has planned for you.

STORY KILLER #1: LIVING SOMEONE ELSE'S STORY

Sometimes our stories get hijacked because we live other people's callings. We admire what someone else is doing, what he or she is accomplishing for God, and we start doing the same thing but without that person's gifts. Our stories become plagiarized copies of someone else's story rather than the masterpieces God originally intended them to be. When we live someone else's story, we don't exercise the gifts God has given us. We don't live out the experiences God wants to put in our path or meet the people He wants us to meet.

The best way to keep a story killer from disrupting your story is to stick to your own story with confidence, knowing that God is a Creator and not a duplicator. He has something uniquely special for each of our lives.

Remember David, the shepherd turned king? He lived out his story with confidence, even when others thought he was being foolish. Here's what happened. When King Saul heard that David was going to fight the giant Goliath, he tried to deter the young man. After all, Goliath was more than nine feet tall. He stood head and shoulders over young David. To top it off, David had not been on a battlefield, and Goliath was a trained mercenary. So Saul told David, *You are not able to go against this Philistine to fight with him; for you are a youth, and he a man of war from his youth.*[1]

Saul had no clue that fighting the giant would be a defining moment in David's life. When Saul tried to dissuade David from challenging Goliath, he had no clue that this was part of the story God designed for David. Had David listened to Saul, his story would have been completely altered. He never would have been celebrated as a giant killer. The nation of Israel would not have been safe from opposing armies and eventually would have lived under enemy occupation by the Philistines. The chain of events designed to prepare David to be king would have been broken.

Seeing David's unwavering determination to fight Goliath, Saul put his own armor on David. *So Saul clothed David with his armor, and he put a bronze helmet on his head; he also clothed him with a coat of mail. David fastened his sword to his armor and tried to walk, for he had not tested them.*[2] David had never been on a battlefield, so the heavy, metal armor must have felt strange.

Saul was a warrior, and in his heyday, he'd killed thousands in battle. His armor was tried and true. Saul wanted David to fight the way he fought. Saul put his story on loan to David. But David's story was different. David said to Saul, *"I cannot walk with these, for I have not tested them." So David took them off.*[3]

Sometimes we fall into the trap of comparing our lives to others. It is easy to think that others have better lives than we do. We assume that if we just copy what someone else does, our lives will be as great, and therein lies the problem. The people whose lives we try to imitate are using their own gifts to fulfill the assignments God has given them. It is not that God loves them more and has given them better lives; it is that they are living out their stories in the way God intends. Because they are using their gifts, abilities, and resources to mirror and represent the image of God, they have found satisfaction and fulfillment.

If David had taken on Saul's armor, he would have been outmaneuvered in the fight. With no armor, David was exposed greatly, but this weakness was actually his strength. Goliath made the fatal mistake of thinking that David was not a danger to him and an easy target. He overlooked the skill David had with a slingshot, so his guard was down. *[David] took his staff in his hand; and he chose for himself five smooth stones from the brook, and put them in a shepherd's bag, in a pouch which he had, and his sling was in his hand.*[4] David put a rock in his sling and brought down the shot. David, the lowly shepherd boy, became a giant slayer that day. He was living the story that God had created him to live, doing what God had created him to do.

Had David worn Saul's armor and slain the giant, God would not have received the glory. No one would have been talking about what God did through David; they would have been talking about what Saul's armor did for David. Saul's armor was state of the art and the best money could buy. It would have been all about the equipment. The front-page news would have pictured the king and David with the armor. The armor might even have been put on display in a museum for people to look at. Armor sales would have gone through the roof! The glory of God would have been stolen. The honor to God would have been swallowed up. That is the problem with adopting someone else's story: It can rob people from seeing what God can do in spite of our humanity. When people see God working in spite of our circumstances, it overwhelms them with one thing: God. This awe is called worship because it gives glory to God and so clearly reflects His image.

David's story demonstrates that ordinary people can accomplish extraordinary things, not because they are smart or lucky but because they are living the stories they were created to live. When God rewrites your story, He will use the skills and opportunities He has given you so you can best mirror and represent His image to the world. If you wish for someone else's experiences and copy someone else's gifts, it will keep you away from the power of your story and potentially rob God of the glory due Him.

Mike is another person who was not seduced into living out someone else's story. Mike has given his life to live and minister in many countries where freedom of religion is restricted or not practiced at all. Government officials who wanted to stop him from doing what God had called him to do persecuted him time after time. Mike was beaten many times and left for dead. He was robbed, imprisoned, and hurt on many occasions.

One day I (Bruce) asked him, "What is it like to suffer greatly?" He looked me square in the face and replied, "Suffer? What are you talking about, I haven't suffered!"

I said, "But, Mike, you have been beaten multiple times for helping people in Third World countries and showing people the love of God. Of course you've suffered!"

Just as fierce was his reply: "That really is not suffering."

Mike lived the story God had for him, and even though he'd been beaten, lived in poverty, and bore the physical scars of a sacrificial life, he lived with a deep sense of satisfaction and fulfillment. He could have cushioned his life by going back to his family's multimillion-dollar business, but then he would have been living his father's story and not his own. He did not veer from what God called him to do. He did not want to squander his gifts, abilities, and resources. He used them all to reflect God's image and glory. He spent his life well. That's what enabled Mike to live a heroic life. His life not only inspired me but also thousands of other ordinary, run-of-the-mill people who are now living in a similar manner.

The ultimate tragedy of copying another person's story is never living out our own. Your story really is better; you just may not know it yet. Pretense is at the core of a stolen story. It is a child's dress-up party, wasting through people, relationships, and time that could be spent living out the real thing. A stolen story is a powerless story because God has not called you to it. God only gives His power to live the story He has given you.

David and Mike confidently lived out their own stories rather than someone else's, and it changed the rest of their lives as well as the stories of countless other people. That's the power of living the story God has for you!

STORY KILLER #2: DISTRACTIONS

Distractions are also powerful story killers. Although you may want God's story, distractions will con you into thinking you can easily add in other commitments.

Have you ever known people God used in extraordinary ways? They accomplish more than the average person. With great ease, they go to the next level in their marriage, career, finances, and major life matters. These people aren't degreed in religion or from a certain background; they simply have learned the secret of focusing on the stories they were created for. You can learn to do the same.

All of us are surrounded by legitimate needs, making it easy for us to get sidetracked doing good things. Problem is, these good things may not be the things God uniquely created us to do. For that reason, we must master the ability to stay focused on fulfilling our purposes. Distractions and busyness constantly pull us away from the story God has for us. Clutter is the enemy of purpose.

Jesus can be our example for how to stay on the path. No one has ever lived a more focused life than He. Jesus made every day count. He measured each moment. His life commitments were not cluttered, despite His having a constant stream of invitations and opportunities. He knew exactly how to handle each of them. Anything outside of His calling never made it on His agenda.

Jesus set definite boundaries for Himself. He could have made His home in a notable nation, but he lived in Palestine, a little country no larger than Connecticut. The Savior of the world confined himself to this small, unimpressive corner of the earth.[5] So insignificant was this area that most of the more well-known rabbis of his day never frequented it. Jesus could have traveled to faraway lands, scattering the gospel over a wider audience, but by narrowing His focus, He was able to pour His life into a small group of people. Jesus' goal was not just to produce believers but also to produce disciples who could carry out ministry in His name.

For thirty years, He remained focused on the family business, pouring His time and energy into a dingy carpenter's shop, again staying on track with the story that His heavenly Father had for Him. Imagine Jesus' taking orders for kitchen cabinets or listening to complaints from dissatisfied customers. He could have thought, *There must be better things for Me to do than make dining room sets!* But He didn't. Nor did He have difficulty confining Himself to such limits, even though He was the Son of God. He knew that was the position God had asked Him to take. He had already become a man — so what were four walls in a carpenter shop? This narrowness would lay the foundation for a public ministry that would turn the world upside down.

Once free from managing the family business, among the thousands of good things He could have done, Jesus confined Himself to the one thing He believed His heavenly Father had given Him to do: *to seek and to save that which was lost.*[6] Such narrowness was hard for others to understand. People were always urging Him to do something grand, such as create an earthly kingdom.

One day while Jesus was teaching, a man from the crowd stepped forward and interrupted Him, saying, *Teacher, tell my brother to divide the inheritance with me.*[7] Story killers often enter our lives when we are just hitting our stride in fulfilling our purposes. Out of nowhere, distractions pop up that are capable of derailing us. Many times the distractions are not bad things. For a brief moment, we are tempted to pursue something good versus fulfilling our true purpose. Not Jesus. His response gives insight into His singular focus: *Man, who made Me a judge or an arbitrator over you?*[8] However good this request might have been, Jesus did not fulfill it because it was not His to do.

Jesus models the secret to setting boundaries. His choice always was to narrow the focus — to harness all His time, energy, and passion in the one thing He was called to do. No one can do everything. No one should attempt everything. This world is broken, and there are a thousand things that need to be done to restore hope. Yet no one, even the best multitasker, can perform them all. Saying yes to every request lessens our impact. It dilutes our purposes. The world will get a greater glimpse of hope and restoration when we stay focused on the stories God gives us.

As image bearers, we are not free to live for our own whims. We do not have the option of thinking or doing whatever we want. Jesus walked the narrow path, and He invites us to join Him on the journey: *Enter through the narrow gate. For wide is the gate and broad is the road that leads to destruction, and many enter through it. But small is the gate and narrow the road that leads to life, and only a few find it.*[9]

The Son of God limited Himself in His earthly ministry. His focus was so razor-sharp that He did not veer from the assignments given to Him by His Father. His service to humankind included a heavy wooden cross, three wrought-iron nails, and a crown of thorns. Has there ever been a more extravagant act of obedience? Has there ever been a more purposeful, sacrificial life?

So when Christ calls us to choose the narrow path, when He calls us to pick up our cross and follow Him, it is sheer foolishness to skip down the trail of overcommitment, trod down the road of busyness, or stroll down the lane of selfishness.

What our culture calls "normal" often requires being over-committed, involved in everything, and saying yes to anyone who demands our time. One sport for the kids is no longer any good, so we involve ourselves year-round in as many things as we can cram into our overtaxed schedule. One hobby is no longer satisfying, so we pursue with all our passion something else that catches our attention, without a single subtraction from the schedule.

The new normal creates distractions, fatigue, heartache, sleepless nights, and trophies that over time are put in the attic. This busyness has no great payoff other than to occupy our time and steal our energy. Cluttered lives are the recipe for inconsistency. An overburdened schedule does nothing for eternity, and it gets us no closer to becoming who God created us to be.

So how do you do it all? The answer is that you don't! In fact, you can't and still fulfill your story. The great news is that sticking to your purpose brings clarity to life. It shows you which activities are essential and which aren't. Try out one of these four options the next time you get the itch to add something else to your life:

- **Drop it**—Subtract something before you add something. Take away something and give more attention to the assignments God gives you.
- **Delegate it**—Invite someone to own the project, event, or obligation.
- **Defer it**—Wait to give a response until you have thought and prayed about it.
- **Dedicate time**—Spend time doing only things that are a part of your assignment.

When we are consistent in saying no to lesser things, our single-mindedness becomes the vehicle for gaining a larger story and thus increasing the impact of our stories on a broken world. These four choices—to drop, delegate, defer, or dedicate—will disentangle you from a cluttered life. They will, in fact, free you to live the story God has for you.

YOU BE YOU

God is counting on you to be His representative. By design, you are His image bearer, and everyone around you needs to see something of His character in you. His plan for you is so much bigger than you could make up on your own or borrow from someone else. Your story has been years in the making, even before you were born. The people in your circle of influence are not there by accident; they were placed there to intersect with your life and be touched by your story. The experiences you've gone through have shaped you for this moment. You have the ability to mirror and represent God in every season of your life and in every circumstance.

Each time you forgive an offender, God's eternal mercy and grace are on display for a world in desperate need of forgiveness and wholeness. Forgiveness releases you from the past and launches you into your future.

Each time you are generous, you are reflecting God's graciousness and love toward you. Each time you extend time, money, energy, and resources in a generous manner to those in need, you are acting as God's representative on their behalf.

Each time you complete a God-given assignment, it not only brings purpose to your life but also helps others see that true satisfaction and fulfillment are attainable.

Each time you act and respond to people in humility, you are mirroring the great sacrifice and humility of Jesus Christ.

And when you trust God in the midst of suffering, His glory and might are visible for a watching world.

Through each of these five life opportunities, you are reflecting and representing the image of God to those who need to know Him. As you do, God is able to exchange your story for His story for you.

That is why you must be you! To live any other way is to blow off God as your Creator. There is not another person on the face of this earth who is more equipped than you to make a difference in your world because no one else has been given your story. It is one of a kind, and it is essential for healing a broken world.

God wants to begin transforming you into the person He created you to be. He can use every experience, joy, heartache, and delay to rewrite your story. Each is equally important to the growth of who you are. Life will never be completely satisfying until you become who God designed you to be and begin making the contribution you have been uniquely gifted to make.

Live life as the image bearer you are.

NOTES

Chapter 2: The Rescue

1. Genesis 3:6.
2. Romans 5:12.
3. Genesis 4:7.
4. Isaiah 59:12.
5. Jeremiah 14:7.
6. Jeremiah 5:25, MSG.
7. See John 4:1-42.
8. Ephesians 1:7, NLT.
9. Galatians 1:5, MSG.
10. M. R. DeHaan, *Broken Things: Why We Suffer* (Grand Rapids, MI: Discovery House, 1948), 60.

Chapter 3: Reflecting the Image of God

1. Genesis 1:27.
2. For the entire Creation account, read Genesis 1.
3. Philippians 1:6, NKJV.
4. www.census.gov/main/www/popclock.html.
5. Psalm 139:1-4, NKJV.
6. See John 8:1-11.
7. John 8:4-5, NKJV.
8. John 8:7.

9. John 8:10-11.

10. John 8:11, NKJV.

11. Romans 8:31, NKJV.

12. Jeremiah 29:11, NKJV.

13. Genesis 1:28.

Chapter 4: Representing the Image of God

1. Anthony A. Hoekema, *Created in God's Image* (Grand Rapids, MI: Eerdmans, 1986), 73.

2. Genesis 2:19-20.

3. Colossians 3:17, NLT.

4. Although everyone who displays creativity gives evidence of being created in the image of God, not everyone does so with God's glory in mind. We all represent God because He is sovereignly working His plan to glorify Himself through humankind, whether we know it or not. The believer has the distinct blessing of being God's ambassador by helping reconcile a lost world back to God through Jesus (see 2 Corinthians 5:19-20). Anthony Hoekema's book *Created in God's Image* gives detailed explanation of reflecting and representing God's image.

5. Ephesians 3:20, MSG.

6. John 9:6-7, NKJV.

7. http://marshill.com/media/genesis/creation-day-6.

8. Genesis 1:28; 2:15.

9. Galatians 6:1-3, MSG.

10. Ephesians 2:10.

11. Matthew 6:1-4.

12. Matthew 5:43-48.

13. Romans 12:20-21.

14. James 2:14-16, NLT.

15. 1 Peter 4:10.

16. 2 Corinthians 5:18.

17. Romans 13:9-10.

18. Ephesians 6:7-8.

19. Matthew 25:34-40.

Chapter 5: Rewriting Your Story Through Forgiveness

1. Matthew 6:9-13.
2. Matthew 6:14-15.
3. R. T. Kendall, *Total Forgiveness* (Lake Mary, FL: Charisma House, 2002), 69.
4. Kendall, 69.
5. Psalm 103:12, ESV.
6. Kendall, 74.
7. Kendall, 71.
8. Matthew 5:7, NLT.
9. Philippians 4:13, NKJV.
10. Luke 7:39.
11. Luke 7:41-43, NLT.
12. Luke 6:27-28, NLT.
13. Kendall, 28.
14. Matthew 5:44-45.
15. Kendall, 74–75.
16. See Genesis 37–45.

Chapter 6: Rewriting Your Story Through Fulfilling Your Assignments

1. 1 Corinthians 2:9, NKJV.
2. Ephesians 2:10.
3. Psalm 31:19, NLT.
4. Genesis 39:2,21,23.
5. 2 Timothy 3:16-17.
6. Romans 14:13.
7. 1 Peter 3:11.
8. Psalm 119:37.
9. Genesis 41:40, NASB.
10. Genesis 41:56-57, NASB.

Chapter 7: Rewriting Your Story Through Generosity

1. Luke 9:24, NLT.
2. Psalm 23:5-6, NKJV.
3. Psalm 103:2, NLT.

4. Psalm 68:19, NKJV.

5. Acts 20:35, NKJV.

6. Mark 10:45.

7. Titus 3:5-6, NLT.

8. 2 Corinthians 9:6-8.

9. Luke 21:1-2, NKJV.

10. Luke 21:3-4, NKJV.

11. Proverbs 3:9-10, NLT.

12. John 3:16, ESV.

13. Luke 6:38, NKJV.

Chapter 8: Rewriting Your Story Through Humility

1. 1 Samuel 16:11, NKJV.

2. 1 Samuel 16:11, NKJV.

3. 1 Samuel 16:12, NKJV.

4. Arthur W. Pink, *The Life of David* (Ann Arbor, MI: Baker, 1981), 24.

5. 1 Samuel 16:7, NKJV.

6. John G. Butler, *David: The King of Israel*, Bible Biography Series, vol. 15 (Clinton, IA: LBC Publications, 1998), 32.

7. 1 Peter 5:5, NKJV.

8. Colossians 3:23-24.

9. 1 Samuel 17:15, NKJV.

10. Philippians 2:3-8.

11. 1 Samuel 17:26, NKJV.

12. 1 Samuel 17:34-37.

13. Luke 16:10.

14. 1 Samuel 17:45,47.

15. 1 Samuel 17:49-51, NKJV.

16. 1 Peter 5:5-6, ESV.

Chapter 9: Rewriting Your Story Through Suffering

1. Hebrews 4:15, NLT.

2. M. R. DeHaan, *Broken Things: Why We Suffer* (Grand Rapids, MI: Discovery House, 1948), 23.

3. Psalm 46:1, NLT.

4. Charles J. Rolls, *The World's Greatest Names* (Neptune, NJ: Loizeaux Brothers, 1984), 29.

5. Psalm 51:17, NKJV.

6. Psalm 34:18, NASB.

7. 2 Corinthians 8:2-4, MSG.

8. Psalm 147:3, NKJV.

9. Psalm 144:2.

10. Psalm 142:5, NKJV.

11. 2 Corinthians 1:3,5.

12. Psalm 23:6, NKJV.

13. John 9:2.

14. John 9:3.

15. See John 9:6-7.

16. DeHaan, 16.

17. Psalm 103:3.

18. Rolls, 31.

19. 1 Corinthians 15:54-55.

20. Romans 8:28, NKJV.

21. DeHaan, 12.

22. Psalm 31:19, NLT.

23. 2 Corinthians 1:4, NLT.

24. Charles J. Rolls, *The Name Above Every Name* (Neptune, NJ: Loizeaux Brothers, 1965), 109.

25. Revelation 21:4, NLT.

26. DeHaan, 61.

27. Colossians 3:10, NLT.

28. Ephesians 4:22-24.

29. 2 Corinthians 4:16-18.

30. L. B. Cowman, *Streams in the Desert* (Grand Rapids, MI: Zondervan, 1997), 375.

31. 1 Peter 4:12-13.

32. 2 Timothy 2:12, NKJV.

33. James 1:12.

34. Romans 8:16-18, NLT.

35. Cowman, 375.

Chapter 10: Story Killers

1. 1 Samuel 17:33, NKJV.
2. 1 Samuel 17:38-39, NKJV.
3. 1 Samuel 17:39, NKJV.
4. 1 Samuel 17:40, NKJV.
5. Charles E. Jefferson, *The Character of Jesus* (New York: Thomas Y. Crowell, 1908), 108.
6. Luke 19:10, NKJV.
7. Luke 12:13, NKJV.
8. Luke 12:14, NKJV.
9. Matthew 7:13-14.

ABOUT THE AUTHORS

Bruce and Heather Moore made the most radical decision of their lives, leaving a large suburb church to rebirth a dying church. Their journey has left nothing untouched in their lives. Their book *Rewritten: Exchanging Your Story for God's Story* is changing the way people think about how God transforms people's futures. As engaging communicators, Bruce is the lead pastor at Christ Fellowship (Tampa, Florida), and Heather speaks at women's conferences all across the country. Christ Fellowship is a diverse and rapidly expanding gathering of Christ followers committed to changing this world for good.

Bruce and Heather are available for consulting and speaking at churches, colleges, and conferences on issues of spiritual growth, church growth, and church planting.

Connect with Bruce at www.1year2live.com and Heather at www.bheathermoore.com.

Regarding a speaking or consulting opportunity, contact Bruce and Heather at speaking@christfellowshiptampa.com.

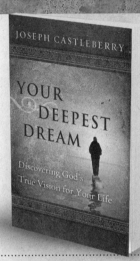